"Paul Remack tackles the often emotional and complex issue of Wealth Transfer and Distribution by simplifying the process and easing the reader into taking action today. For people who have wanted to plan ahead but didn't know the necessary steps, here is a guide that shares the process in everyday English."

DAN CLEVELAND
Executive Director of Major & Planned Gifts

*"Paul has shared a wealth of knowledge based on decades of experience in a readable and entertaining book. **Playing the Game** is a must read for everyone who wants to provide for their family."*

JOHN SCHULTZ, former CFO

"Paul Remack has identified the core problem of successful business people. They are focused on their business. Hence, this book addresses the problem we all face. What happens next? Most of us have little interest in tax codes or what lawyers and accountant said, so we postpone these discussions because so many other issues seem more important or urgent. aul develops a roadmap for the disinterested, too busy-to-focus successful family who wants a plan but doesn't like planning."

BOB SKERKER, Business Owner/Philanthropist

*"Paul Remack writes with insight, experience, and great compassion for people who—without his expert guidance—could easily make million-dollar mistakes. If you have assets of any significance, and if you have heirs or a favorite charity you want to pass them on to, then you owe it to yourself to read **Playing the Game**."*

MICHAEL LEVIN, *New York Times* bestselling author

"I read the book and I thought it was fantastic! I also appreciated the quality and usefulness of the notes section."

ALEX PAMPALONE, Senior Director of Development

"You told us over and over that our cooperation was not the average but rather uncommon,and cooperation allows greater flexibility and increased benefit."

LANCE PORTER, business owner/multi-generational company

"Great, really great."

JOHN CARVER, former Executive VP, Human Resources and Philanthropist

"Thank you for sharing this text related to your and Phil's relationship and mutual hard work. I think that it is very well-written."

KATHIE BUCHANAN, Venture Capitalist/Entrepreneur

"Paul's book is very timely for those of us who have procrastinated when thinking about the distribution of our assets. Paul has made tremendous strides, on our behalf, by informing us through easy to understand examples. He goes further by providing links to more reading material just at the perfect moment when our brains tell us to do additional research on a topic or issue."

WALTER HARROWER, CFO and Public Accountant

"What Remack has written is winning and valuable reading."

GREG CASTILLO, Entrepreneur/Caregiver

"While the text provides straightforward, understandable discussion of the issues, the true benefit of the book may lie in the chapter end notes, clearly pointing the way to further information about specific topics."

ALAN DUDAS, Engineer

"Remack's examples take women's concerns into consideration and speak clearly to everyday issues and problems affecting women. Anyone with an investment account, a retirement plan, or a house can benefit from Paul's thoughtful and caring writing. You don't need to be rich to get a lot from this book."

CHERYL DEWORKIN, business owner

"I think it's really cool that Paul Remack undertook this project and I think that it will be very helpful for readers. I reflected that Playing the Game seems to be the generous sharing of his expertise and experience gained over time, together with his usual candor."

TOM FAIR, real estate investor

Playing the Game

playing the game

CREATE YOUR LEGACY AND PRESERVE YOUR ESTATE FOR FUTURE GENERATIONS

PAUL REMACK

NEW YORK

NASHVILLE • MELBOURNE • VANCOUVER

Playing the Game

Create Your Legacy and Preserve Your Estate for Future Generations

Published in New York, New York, by Morgan James Publishing. Morgan James is a trademark of Morgan James, LLC. www.MorganJamesPublishing.com

The Morgan James Speakers Group can bring authors to your live event. For more information or to book an event visit The Morgan James Speakers Group at www.TheMorganJamesSpeakersGroup.com.

ISBN 9781683505655 paperback
ISBN 9781683505662 eBook
Library of Congress Control Number: 2017906777

Cover Design by:
Megan Whitney
megan@creativeninjadesigns.com

Interior Design by:
Chris Treccani
www.3dogcreative.net

In an effort to support local communities, raise awareness and funds, Morgan James Publishing donates a percentage of all book sales for the life of each book to Habitat for Humanity Peninsula and Greater Williamsburg.

Get involved today! Visit
www.MorganJamesBuilds.com

Contents

Acknowledgements

n the process of gathering my thoughts for this book, it became clear how much I owe to many people. In all honesty, I can't come close to acknowledging all those who deserve credit for the inspiration and motivation they contributed. Most of the help I received was positive; *however*, some of the greatest inspiration came from people—especially clients—who fought me over the need to "play the game." Nothing sharpens my thoughts and inspires my efforts more than being told "no." Rejection made me go back and work harder to make my propositions clearer and more concise. Thankfully, these people forced me to reconsider my thought process and to become better at everything I did. To all those naysayers who never became clients, and to those clients who initially took the position that my planning recommendations were unnecessary, unworkable, or a waste of time, I say, "Thank you!" Their insistence that the game didn't apply to them, or that they would deal with their issues later, forced me to become better at my profession. They motivated me to address issues differently and to work at making the game understandable.

While those who fought me provided critical perspective, the families who acknowledged and embraced the game were obviously more important. In working with them, I enjoyed the opportunity to apply my knowledge to real-life situations, which provided a different motivation: the motivation to learn how to do things the right way. Their experiences provided me with the basis for the insights I've shared in this book. They moved me from conjecture to action, and it was the heat of their experience that delivered these time-tested results. It has been my pleasure to work with some of these client families for more than thirty years, and the length and depth of these relationships has enabled me to see how the game has changed during that time.

As important as the client families were, working with other professional advisors further helped me to refine my approach and delivery. While my clients provided the raw material, working with fellow professionals compelled me to see how others thought the game should be played. There were times when we had differences, although more often than not, we came to the same conclusions, even when we took different paths to get there. By examining differences in attitude and approach, I honed my skill at playing the game. While many of my fellow advisors made their mark on my approach to the game, I want to recognize a special few who contributed most to my thoughts: Linda Slider, Steve Anderson, Jeff Rollert, Lance Porter, Sam Cohen, Ed Hanley, Jane Allen-Morin, Ed Gardner, Hal Porter, Steve Shelton, Mike Fitzgerald, Bob Skerker, Jon Allen, Ruth Hurshman, Peter Siewert, Charles Bellig, and Bart Mowry. Each of these fellow professionals influenced me in ways that are difficult to describe but impossible to ignore. To each of them, a grateful tip of the hat!

Beyond these groups was one other small but influential collection of individuals: my mentors. Three friends particularly stand out as major influences in my development as an advisor and a thinker: Joe Feigenbaum, John Carver, and Albert Horn. Each of these gentlemen, consummate professionals in their individual areas of expertise, helped me realize my ability to see and play the game. To say that they shaped my thinking and my philosophy would be an understatement. Each of them challenged me in ways too complicated to share here. What can be said is that I came away from our time together with the genesis of many of the ideas in this book. For this, I offer my gratitude and appreciation.

At the same time, bringing these thoughts and experiences to print required steady hands who not only were willing to assist me but believed in what I was presenting. I want to thank Michael Levin and Bryan Gage. While Michael assisted me by taking the long view of what could be, Bryan rolled up his sleeves and slogged through my materials with his scalpel and cleaver. Bryan was a wonderful editor for this project, and a wizard at wordsmithery. I'd also like to thank the publishing team at Morgan James for turning my manuscript into a thoughtful and well-designed book. Kudos to David Hancock for assembling a first-rate team!

Finally, and with my most heartfelt appreciation, I want to thank my beloved wife, Linda. I owe so much of who I am today to her. She has been my manager, coach, and muse from the day we met in 2001. She has guided me with her love, her wisdom, her kindness, and—most important for a roughneck like me—her gentleness. Without her, I would have never considered writing this book. Coming home to her and to the various cats that have graced our home over the years (Cat, Chryssy, and Gracie) has always been gratifying after a long day of playing the game.

Obviously, despite all this help and inspiration, I have still not completely mastered the game. To the extent that there are errors in what I have presented, they are mine and mine alone. Despite my best efforts, I still have much to learn.

Finally, I know that you will play the game of Wealth Transfer and Distribution whether you want to or not; I hope you benefit from what I have presented in these pages, and that you will choose to play the game to the best of your ability.

Thank you!

Chapter 1

Introduction to the Game

———————◆———————

I f you're financially successful, then you're to be congratulated. You've worked hard to earn your success, and having achieved it, you're likely to spend the remainder of your days in relative comfort and security if you use your money wisely.

But despite all the wealth you've earned, if you think you've ensured the comfort and security of your children and grandchildren, you'd better think again. As unthinkable and discouraging as it may be, it is possible that your children or grandchildren may one day lack financial security.

Consider the case of shipping and railroad magnate Cornelius Vanderbilt, one of the richest men in American history. By the time of his death in 1877, Vanderbilt had accumulated a personal fortune of more than $100 billion in today's dollars. And in 1973 a family reunion brought together 120 of Vanderbilt's direct descendants—not one of whom was a millionaire.[1]

Under the corrosive onslaught of the imprudent choices made by several generations of Vanderbilt's descendants, the family fortune dissolved like a baby tooth left in a glass of Coca-Cola.[2] This is what can happen to successful people who fail to understand that wealth transfer and distribution, just like wealth acquisition, is a game. If you play the game badly—or worse, if you

1

don't understand that you *are* playing a game—then your heirs could lose much of what you've worked all your life to provide for them.[3]

But it needn't be this way. I can help you learn to see wealth transfer for the game it is, and I can help you understand how that game is played and won.

———————— ♦ ————————

I have been a financial advisor for more than thirty years. During that time my approach has focused on the value of planning—specifically on the use of legal, tax, accounting, and strategic techniques. I have also changed my approach and thinking more than a few times over these years in response to changes in the planning environment. Today I specialize in multigenerational planning and work almost exclusively as chief financial officer to high-net-worth families. As such, I am responsible for each family's financial health and well-being. I always work directly with the family's leaders, and my compensation is fee driven. I am a Professional Fiduciary in California, and as such, I am obliged to put the client's interest first. Would you expect anything less from your personal CFO?

Mom & Pop Millionaires

During my time as an advisor, I have worked primarily with families whose fortunes came from real estate and family business interests, and then—after some liquidity event (e.g., the sale of a business interest or land parcel)—stocks, bonds, and cash. Most of these client families are self-made, the products of the economic good times that propelled America to its standing as an economic giant after World War II. Many of these families have mastered the art of wealth preservation, but many have not. Those who failed, at least in my experience, failed because they chose to isolate themselves after achieving their success, without considering how to move their success downstream to their children and grandchildren.

The successful families, on the other hand, understood that no matter how much they worked, planned, and succeeded, their work would never be done. Just as important, they realized that their business efforts alone would not ensure their success. While these families were good at what they did, they knew that their financial success required outside support and assistance: They needed a team to assist them in their efforts.

My typical client family is the first-generation success story—the classic "Mom & Pop" who took the family from a comfortable middle-class lifestyle to a more successful upper-class environment, at least on the family's personal financial statement. While they added zeroes to their personal net worth, they generally maintained understated lifestyles designed to downplay their success. In many ways my client families are the now-famous "millionaires next door" profiled in the book by Thomas J. Stanley and William D. Danko[4]—families who have grown financially but maintained modest lifestyles, disguising their financial success.

For decades I have watched as personal balance sheets have doubled, tripled, and quadrupled while Mom and Dad maintained their perspective on life. These observations have been made possible by the relationships I have been fortunate enough to maintain with my earliest client families, and they have enabled me to see the results of my work over the course of several generations. This, in turn, has given me insight into why some families succeed in passing their assets to subsequent generations while other, equally successful families fail to deliver on this obligation.

How did these families achieve their initial success? They worked hard, gave their business efforts serious consideration, and learned to communicate successfully, at least on a business level. As a group, they enjoyed narrow but sharp focus. This is not to say that they didn't make mistakes, but they learned quickly from their mistakes because they understood what they were doing. In fact, these successful families often assumed a degree of risk in business activities that seemed disproportionate to their normal risk tolerance. But they did so because they understood the risk of their endeavors. In fact, their attitude toward business decisions had a special quality to it—almost that of a game.

For these families, business became a personal playground where they knew they could have fun while they succeeded. Work became play, and as players, they came to understand that there were rules and limits . . . but they also understood that these rules and limits were elastic and changeable.

Eventually, many of these first-generation families begin to look beyond their business accomplishments to see what else was possible. While their business expertise grew, these families often came to points of indecision and confusion when operating outside their narrow areas of expertise. And when the time came to determine how they would pass their assets to future generations, these client families came to realize that they were moving into new, uncomfortable, and unknown areas.

Today the US is in the midst of the largest wealth transfer ever—as much as $40 trillion is expected to change hands over the next thirty years.[5] However, while this is newsworthy today, twenty years ago there was an earlier "largest wealth transfer ever" of $15 trillion. I expect that barring some economic cataclysm, twenty years from now there will be a still bigger wealth transfer. In other words, what we are experiencing today has happened before, and likely will occur again in the future.

But the process itself doesn't change. The challenge of working outside of our areas of expertise remains. For successful families today, the challenge is the same as it was twenty years ago—namely, how to create an environment in which the hard-won success of one generation can be transferred and distributed to succeeding generations with a high degree of surety.

A Different Approach—Wealth Transfer as a Game

The wealth transfer of the 1990s was hampered by severe economic conditions early in this century, which curtailed both its impact and its duration. With the NASDAQ crash of 2001–2002, the real estate collapse of 2006–2008, and the Great Recession of 2008–2009, enormous amounts of money evaporated, and the potential springboard effect was lost for many of those earlier transfers that had begun during the nineties. I saw several families move outside of their safety zones and try to become what they weren't, with mostly negative outcomes. This pattern of behavior took many forms: a successful insurance brokerage owner deciding to become a venture capitalist, a successful venture capitalist trying to become a real estate magnate, an equipment-rental owner fancying himself a vineyard expert. The resulting financial dilution was exacerbated by estate tax policies, which confiscate wealth if they are not properly anticipated. I witnessed an heir taking hours to sign a check for $10 million in payment of estate taxes, while both faulting his parents for insufficient planning and promising himself that he would not repeat their mistake.

Happily, most of the client families I serve were able to avoid these issues. In many instances, they benefitted from not being ready to transfer because they were too young; they were still in the accumulation phase of life and their children weren't old enough to receive their inheritances. These families maintained their wealth in assets they understood.

While there were client families who successfully managed the transfer/distribution issue, they succeeded because they put in the time and effort—often grudgingly—to identify and solve impending problems. These client families delivered their wealth intact to their heirs and created an environment in which the children of the first-generation owners assumed an active role in the planning process and often actually identified the need for forward thinking. Three of my first client families recognized the threats embodied in the transfer/distribution process and managed to deliver their entire estates to succeeding generations without dilution. Why? Why didn't they suffer the kinds of losses other families endured? I believe these families succeeded because they learned to play the wealth-transfer game the same way they'd played the wealth-acquisition game that had made them successful in the first place. They applied the discipline and determination that they'd used to acquire their wealth in the first place and made playing the game integral to their management of their wealth transfer.

These successful families had the same information as everyone else, but they succeeded by taking different approaches. When they went outside the comfortable confines of their familiar business environments, they adopted the attitude that each activity has its own set of rules and regulations. Accordingly, they spent time and effort investigating ways to bend and massage these limits to their advantage.

In sports, when players achieve mastery of the game, they often say that the game slows down and that they can see everything on the field (this is the state of mind that athletes call "being in the zone"). It is my position that these families slowed the game of Wealth Transfer and Distribution to the point at which they could see the entire field of play and all the action on it.

The purpose of this book is to help other successful families do what these families have done. My goal is to identify the requirements of successful wealth transfer and distribution, and to break down the necessary components in order to provide a framework that allows families to transfer and distribute wealth more effectively and more efficiently, irrespective of the changing rules and regulations that often threaten to undermine even the best decisions.

Why do I believe I can provide these insights? What makes me confident that I see something meriting discussion and consideration? My success in helping families since 1982. I know my clients have benefitted from my expertise because they and their other professional advisors have said so. In teaching them how play the game as well as it can be played, I have introduced my clients to new ways of thinking and planning.

From the City of Homes to the Golden State

I grew up in Berwyn, Illinois, a largely blue-collar suburb of Chicago known as the "City of Homes." Growing up, the last thing I ever thought that I would be was a financial advisor. Kids like me didn't aspire to much more than working in downtown Chicago and moving further into the suburbs. That was probably as good as it would ever get.

But fate and luck proved me wrong. After graduating from high school, I received a partial academic scholarship from Bradley University, where I majored in history and graduated with honors. After Bradley, I was fortunate to receive a fellowship from the University of Southern California to pursue a PhD in Renaissance history. My time at USC was incredibly valuable; it taught me to think, write, and speak critically.

After finishing graduate school in the late 1970s, I began working for a family-owned boutique publisher in the San Francisco area, where I found myself faced with the question of what to do next. In my heart I wanted to be a college basketball coach, but my poor prospects for success in this field led me to choose an alternate career path: financial planning. I realized that, like a college basketball coach, a good financial planner works with highly talented, successful people who have the potential to become stars but need some assistance honing their skills, especially in areas outside their comfort zones. I also realized that success depends on the coordinated efforts of a team of professionals, and that just like a basketball team, these professionals need to come together as strangers and learn to operate *as a team*. In short, I realized that financial planning should be approached like a game.

Unfortunately, the financial advisory business in the early 1980s was not interested in this approach or in my way of thinking. Although I secured interviews, reactions to me and my ideas—and more important, my own reactions to what was expected of me—were negative. I went into these interviews with an innocent expectation that I was going to consult, but the companies that were hiring wanted me to sell. The brokerage houses were looking for someone with a Rolodex of names from which to cull sales opportunities, but I knew no one and had little to offer, and my early attempts at taking my approach to financial-planning firms were met with little success.

Finally, almost out of desperation, I interviewed with Connecticut General (CG). Fortunately, CG had two sales channels: agency and brokerage. Brokerage was made for me. Instead of having to supply a list of names the size of a phonebook, I only needed to cultivate a few professionals in the Property & Casualty business as sources for clients. The idea behind brokerage was that I would become a resource to the clients of the P&C brokers and share financial success (i.e., commissions) with the P&C producers. Here I could add value to successful people based on the transfer of credibility from their trusted advisor (the P&C broker), enabling me to deliver good advice and generate economic success. While my trajectory was not straight-line, it was sufficient that within a few years of hitting the street, my first partner and I decided to leave CG (now CIGNA), and set up our own practice along with five other former CIGNA advisors.

What I gleaned from the CG experience was that my initial assumptions were correct. Being a good advisor *was* like being a basketball coach, except for the fact that the players didn't know how good they were and how much they would benefit from additional coaching. While the business owners were successful within their field of play, they lacked many characteristics necessary for greater success: They tended to be loyal to a fault; even when they outgrew the competency of their advisors, they stuck with them. They didn't realize that their needs exceeded their advisors' ability to deliver, and they had limited expectations of what an advisor should provide. Most of these early clients thought their accountants were great if they prepared taxes on a timely basis, and that their attorneys were terrific if they didn't call with any problems or questions.

Anyone coming in with new or different ideas was immediately suspect. The common response was, "If I needed to know this, my attorney or accountant would have told me." To say that there was little curiosity about new ideas would be an understatement. Consequently, I adopted a very low-key approach and sought first to determine whether the basics were covered. I didn't discuss powers of attorney or investments unless clients showed an interest in funding an IRA or making a retirement-plan deposit. Even at this very basic level of discussion, however, brokers and their clients had glazed eyes thirty minutes into the conversation.

The first few years of this process were full of fits and starts. I was a competent messenger with a great message, but a play needs an audience or the production is doomed to close due to poor ticket sales. Happily, additional impetus came in the form of rising real estate prices in the Bay Area. Suddenly, clients were selling properties and finding themselves with more cash than they could spend. This forced them out of their comfort zones, since they now had more capital at rest than ever before. Successful business owners were finding themselves in a new situation: excess cash and no knowledge of what to do.

It was at this point that the coaching model I wanted to bring to clients began to flower. Working closely with other professionals, I became that old cliché, the planning quarterback for many clients. To maximize my ability to serve my clients, I secured a master of science in taxation from Golden Gate University. Modeled after the famed tax program at New York University, this program suited my purpose: to give me the credibility to work side by side with other professional advisors. Over time I acquired additional credentials: I first became a certified financial planner, and then a registered investment advisor. My goal was to show that I was sensitive to tax issues, and that I was in a position to discuss them in a different way than an accountant or attorney might frame them.

I was slowly developing my distinct, team-oriented approach: I viewed my fellow professionals as coaches, and asked the same of them for me. I moved from being a resource to being a coach. This change set me apart from the retail financial-planning industry, which focused on salespeople and product reps disguised as "consultants." By being in the right place at the right time and by extending my education, I finally found myself where I wanted to be in the late 1980s.

More important, I came to the understanding that has informed my work ever since: that it is all a game. The ability to define and play the game, to be able to use the rules to your advantage, to structure and define the playing field, and finally to build the team best suited to bring home the championship was the logical result. It became clear that what I do is help clients play a game to the best of their ability, taking into account their risk tolerance, their goals and objectives, and their ultimate willingness to play.

Understanding Your Options

Playing the game—effecting the changes necessary to transfer and distribute wealth successfully—is sometimes counterintuitive. It contradicts the old adage, "If it ain't broke, don't fix it." But in playing any game, that adage is a crutch, not an answer. It's too easy to keep doing what works. Change is generally difficult, and change in regard to money matters is especially uncomfortable and often frightening. And yet, without change, my clients would not understand the options that exist to better their own situations and those of their children and grandchildren. Successful wealth transfer and distribution requires openness to new ideas, and to change in general.

There are new ideas and new approaches every year because there are changes to the transfer environment—the field on which the actual game of Wealth Transfer and Distribution is played.[6] In order to determine whether what worked yesterday will work today, it is necessary to continually assess what's new and determine whether it allows the player to improve his results. This is planning's greatest challenge. It is a challenge that must be accepted by any professional advisor worth his or her salt, and by any family that hopes to achieve its goals.

Are you aware of how your options today differ from yesterday's? Can you distinguish what works on an individual basis? Are you ready to challenge yourself and your family with new ideas or approaches? Even the most successful game-playing families are often unaware of the breadth of their choices. Ensuring that every family understands what strategies will deliver the best results is the calling of the competent professional advisor, irrespective of specialty.

The purpose of this book is simple: to teach you to play the game that is played by every person who has assets to enjoy, financial goals to achieve, and plans for her family's future. I want you to understand that there is a game being played, whether you participate or not. This book will explain why certain families succeed in their efforts to pass value downstream, and what is required to create the environment for success. On the other hand, I do not intend to provide how-tos, because the how-tos change over time.

In the pages that follow I will show you how to identify and understand the components necessary to play the game well. I will demonstrate how successful families and individuals can reach their objectives by learning the rules and regulations, by acquiring the right team members, and by understanding that this game is ongoing and subject only to the limits of personal appetite. The game of Wealth Transfer and Distribution is one of the most exciting and satisfying games that can be played. There are no age-based, gender-based, or health-based restrictions on who can play; the game is open to anyone who wants to leave anything of value to an heir, a charity, or any other beneficiary. While there are rules, these rules can be manipulated by players who understand the game and are willing to create their own playing fields. Most of us will play this game; the question is whether we will play this game to the best of our abilities and whether we will accept less than the optimal result. My goal is to help you understand what it takes to play the game well. I can't tell you what specific actions you should take to accomplish your unique goals. But I can provide an understanding of the components necessary for success in your transfers and distributions.

Notes

1. Missy Sullivan, "Lost Inheritance," *Wall Street Journal*, March 8, 2013.
2. Losing money is not limited to only the super-rich; ordinary people run through inheritances and gifts in as little as two years. See Scott Sanders, "Easy Come, Easy Go: Why 35% of Americans Squander Their Inheritance," *Trust Advisor*, November 18, 2015. Also see Juliette Fairley, "The Downside of Sudden Wealth," *Private Wealth*, June 16, 2016.
3. Monopoly is an old-school board game for wealth management; a newer version is Catan, which takes the concepts of resources and making deals much further. See Roland McMillan, "What Board Games Can Teach Your Clients About Wealth Management," *Trust Advisor*, April 1, 2016.
4. Stanley, Thomas, and William Danko, *The Millionaire Next Door* (New York, Pocket Books, 1996).
5. Estimates as to the impending wealth transfer vary from $16 to $40 trillion; for our purposes, I have settled on $40 trillion. See Kenneth Kienoski, CNBC, "How to Manage the Impending $30T Wealth Transfer," *Trust Advisor*, November 16, 2015; Ansuya Harjani, "The Biggest Family Wealth Transfers in History are About to Happen," *Trust Advisor*, CNBC, October 13, 2015.
6. Unfortunately, the gaming environment seems to change on a generational basis, making the search for a static environment quixotic at best. For more detail on generational changes, see writings by Neil Howe and William Strauss. Also see John Mauldin, "Generational Chaos Ahead; Thoughts from the Frontline," *Mauldin Economics*, June 19, 2016.

Chapter 2

Defining the Game

Prologue

To validate the materials that follow, I need to qualify myself as someone who follows his own advice. So here are the facts about the steps that my family has taken that match up with the chapters in this book. I hope that each chapter's prologue will help you find yourself in what I have to say.

When Linda and I defined the game for ourselves in semiretirement and beyond, we identified the following as our goals:

◊ We want to maintain our lifestyle and we want to continue living in our home should either of us become incapacitated.

◊ We want to make sure that when one of us dies, the survivor is left with monetary and advisory resources.[1]

◊ After we both die, we want to deliver assets primarily to family members—but also to charities—at the lowest transfer costs.

◊ We want to avoid mistakes that might endanger our ability to preserve our assets.

My wife has an adult son and an adult grandson from her previous marriage. We are what's becoming the prototypical American family: a blended relationship involving at least one prior marriage and potentially children from that or other relationships. We own a home with a small mortgage as well as other real estate, either directly or as co-investors. We have at least one checking account, a savings account, two pensions, multiple IRA accounts, 401(k) accounts, and a personal investment account as well as other assets. I own a business with employees, and I have a longstanding relationship with another company that I originally founded, from which I am retiring my ownership interest. As far as Linda and I are concerned, we have won the game. Assuming we take good care of what we have, our resources should support us during our lifetimes and help family members and charities when we are gone.

Linda and I meet regularly to discuss where we are and how we are playing the game. When necessary, we modify what we are doing to better reflect what we think we *should* be doing. This can mean changing our trust or will, adding to or reducing the amount of insurance we carry, modifying our investment accounts, and either spending or saving more money. We keep a tally of what we have, what we owe, and where this puts us relative to our goals and objectives. This is how we keep score.[2]

Because we are busy and active, we have built a support team to help us. Our closest advisors are our property and casualty broker, our attorney, and our accountant. Although I am capable of making investment decisions for us, we use investment specialists, including wealth managers and real estate professionals. We believe that we are more likely to reach our goals by not trying to do everything ourselves (although that is an option).

To make sure that we take advantage of opportunities that could help us, we alter our playing field in ways that favor us whenever we can. I apply my tax, insurance, and investment knowledge as often as possible. Since we don't want to be overconfident, we share our thoughts with our specialists and with our attorney and accountant. By asking them to critique what we are doing, we try to anticipate potential shortfalls. So far, our playing field has been tilted in our favor.

Playing both offense and defense is critical for us. Since we started with little, we are very conscientious about how we use funds. When we see opportunities, we try to build our wealth. But we aren't rich, so we must consider adequate protections. When we can, we try to transfer risk. For example, since we have a small home mortgage, we have an insurance policy that will cover its cost if I pass away before we have paid off this debt. If I live a long time and either reduce or pay off the mortgage, then when I do pass, there will be funds remaining in excess of the policy's original purpose (i.e., paying off the mortgage).

We have also played defense by determining how best to accommodate the needs of Linda's son and grandson if she predeceases me. By making use of several advanced techniques, we have created a funded trust designed to help her offspring without depriving me of needed assets. Our goal is to be aggressive when it makes sense, but to be cautious always.

Because we are in our mid-sixties, how we manage our remaining years—the balance of our playing season—is critical. We don't want to reemploy ourselves full time, and we want our money to outlast us. We are moving from a time when accumulation of assets was paramount to a time when the use and transfer of assets starts becoming more important.[3] Thus, we check regularly to ensure that our plans are still on course—and adjust our plans if we are off course. We also share our transfer and distribution plans with family members and other recipients so that they understand their potential interests. Finally, we check regularly with our other team players to make sure they don't think we're missing something.

Since we are subject to the temptations of excess like anyone else, we try to ignore the noise that dominates the news, especially as pertains to financial matters. Our goals are long-term in nature, and therefore potentially at odds with the latest "hot" ideas—but we don't ignore major trends that merit our attention. For example, in 2008–2009, when the US stock market declined significantly, we were fortunate enough to avoid much of the downturn by having a good portion of our funds in cash.

As you will see, almost everything we are doing follows the steps outlined in the chapters of this book. For Linda and me, winning the game is acting consciously in ways that will support us and our lifestyles and leave sufficient money to be distributed to family members and charities. Barring a major catastrophe, we will deliver the balance of what we have at death to our beneficiaries at no tax cost. It is crucial to understand, however, that *there are no guarantees in life* (or in this book). But by playing the game the best we can, we increase our chance for success and happiness.[4]

Transfer vs. Distribution

To be clear, there is a difference between wealth transfer and wealth distribution.[5] Wealth *transfer* is the process through which ownership of an asset is transferred to another person or entity, making that asset subject to our taxation system. Wealth *distribution* occurs when the player actually gives someone something. A transfer often carries with it an actual taxable event (which usually affects the donor), while a distribution—which is usually an after-tax event—occurs when the recipient actually gets something.[6]

For example, I can set up a trust for you today, and even if you don't receive anything from that trust for twenty years, I have still made a transfer.[7] By comparison, wealth *distribution* requires a completed action, like a pass in football. The quarterback throws the ball, the receiver catches it, and a successful play occurs.

There are all sorts of examples of wealth distribution. Simple examples are outright gifts in life or at death. But distribution can also be complicated, such as when a parent forgives a loan to a child, or if Mom and Dad write $10,000 checks to their adult children at Christmas every year. What is important here is that while it is *possible* to make wealth distributions without creating wealth transfers (such as by making a gift, provided the value of the gift is not too high), most significant distributions carry a transfer element.[8]

So the real difference between transfer and distribution is that transfer is the event that creates—or may create—a taxable event.[9] The *effect* of the transfer is the distribution. After the transfer has been subjected to taxation (or found not to be taxable), what's left is distributed. Transfer is what occurs between the donor and the recipient; what the recipient actually receives is the distribution. I may decide to give you a million bucks, but after the tax authority has taken its share, you only see $600,000. I have still *transferred*

$1 million, but the *distribution* is only $600,000. In short, transfer equals gross amount; distribution equals net amount.[10]

The concepts of wealth transfer and distribution will affect almost anyone with assets of value; you don't need to be rich to play the game.[11] With the proliferation of 401(k) accounts and group employee benefits, most workers have something to distribute; for many Americans the family home, even mortgaged, represents their most valuable asset.[12] The ramifications of ownership are simple: *If you own something, you are a player, whether you like or not and whether you realize it or not.*

And just like a pickup basketball game at the corner playground, wealth transfer and distribution has rules and means of scoring, even in the most casual situations. Consequently, it makes sense for each player to understand how the game is played.[13]

Bounding

Because of the wide variation among players—one person may own a family home worth $100,000 and another may have assets worth $30 million—no two families should play the game the same way.[14] What is good for me is not necessarily good for you. Thus, the definition of success varies from person to person.[15] Everyone wants to win, but what people want to win and how they define winning varies.[16]

In addition to personal variation among players, wealth transfer is further complicated by factors such as valuation and timing. Value is determined differently for different kinds of assets. Transferring and distributing a family business is very different from transferring and distributing an investment account, even if the values are exactly the same.[17] If you want to transfer an investment account, you're dealing with hard and fast numbers. The value is what the value is. There are objective outside sources from which you can get a specific numbers. For example, if you own a mutual fund and want to transfer the value of that mutual fund, today's closing prices will tell you the exact value of that mutual fund for today, and you can multiply the share price by the number of shares in order to determine a firm value. No argument.

A business or a piece of real property, on the other hand, often has a range of values, which makes it more challenging to pass on these kinds of assets because of the difficulty of determining their value. If two people go out and evaluate the same business, they are likely to come up with different valuations. Consequently, transferring a business or a piece of property is more complicated than transferring an investment account because the valuation processes are more subjective.

Similarly, timing varies from situation to situation. Baseball is played in innings, soccer in halves, and golf in holes, but the object of each game is to determine a winner. The same is true in wealth transfer and distribution. In some cases, the goal is to accomplish something today; in other cases, twenty years from now. In all cases, however, the end result is measured by a simple concept: winning or losing.

For the reasons above, it is necessary to *bound* the problem. Just as every game has its own rules and time frame, every transfer and distribution has its own players and endgame objective. Bounding the problem, or *defining the game*, means taking time to define goals and objectives.[18] Playing roulette, in which the outcome is immediate, is very different from playing a game of chess, which can takes hours to complete. In roulette, the outcome is immediate gratification or regret. The odds are no better than fifty-fifty (unless you're foolish enough to bet heavily on a particular number), and strategy is an irrelevant concept. Chess, on the other hand, requires strategy and tactics, and often reveals something about each player's personality and appetite for risk.

It is necessary to define the desired result in any game. While winning is a simple way to measure endgame success, the actual identification of *what it means to win* is essential. A game of strategy like chess is much more sophisticated and complex than a game of chance-like roulette. Thus, unless the player wants to rely on the success of a single event (as one does in roulette), it makes sense to take the time to determine first how success will be measured and then how it can best be achieved. Chess and roulette are defined—i.e., bounded—by their respective complexity and simplicity. The objective of each game is the same—to win—but the process by which one gets to this end differs.

The difference between roulette and chess is analogous to the difference between a simple gift and the transfer of a complicated asset whose value may be difficult to pin down. For example, I can give up to $14,000 as an immediate distribution to as many people as I want every year without any tax consequence. It's simple: I write you a check, or I give you cash, or I hand you stock worth $14,000, and it's done. It is a completed transfer, *and* a completed distribution. That may be one of the things I do on an annual basis as part of the game.

On the other hand, if you are my beloved son, I may want you to receive my business at the end of my life, and so I set up a process for handing that business over to you—and *that* game may take thirty years to play. Concurrent with those two games we might even have a third game, because your sister isn't involved in the business and I want to make sure that both of you get approximately equal benefit. And so to that end, I make sure that your sister receives a specific amount of publicly traded stock. Of course, I'm not quite sure yet what the business is going to be worth thirty years from now, and for that matter, neither is anyone else. Likewise, your sister's stock isn't necessarily guaranteed to retain its value. So while I may want you both to receive approximately equal inheritances, I may have to wait thirty years to be sure the distribution goes as originally planned.

How the Players Change over Time

In every family's wealth-transfer game, there are multiple levels of players.[19] There are current players, retired players (either of whom, as we will soon see, can sometimes be the owners), and future players. The owners are the people who create the asset and who subsequently want to transfer and distribute it.[20] In some cases, these people may now be inactive due to withdrawal or death . . . but the game they started continues to this day.

For example, let's assume your grandfather had the foresight to buy a piece of land where your father built the house you now own, in which you now live. The transition from Grandpa to Dad to you is evidence of transfer and distribution over time. But more important, it is evidence of a game being played, whether consciously or unconsciously.[21] In this instance, you are the current player, while your grandpa—the original owner—and your father are retired or former players.

This progression leads us to another important group of players: the future players. After you are gone, who will enjoy this home or benefit from its value? Will it be your children? Their children? A charity? Or will you simply spend the home's value and have the game end with you?[22]

Each group of players has its own characteristics, wants, and needs. In some cases this may mean that the original owner's wishes do not align with the desires of current or future players.[23] It is therefore important to make sure that the team (the original owner, the current player, and the future beneficiary) share enough wants and needs to make the transfer and distribution worthwhile. This amounts to playing well together, which is often necessary in order to play the game successfully.[24] If all players share the same agenda, then success, while not guaranteed, is more probable.[25] Conversely, when players don't see eye to eye, the likelihood of a successful outcome may be diminished (although it is not impossible).[26] Complementary players don't guarantee success, nor do at-odds players forecast failure; but there are patterns that seem to occur over time. The most successful families I have worked with share a sense of commitment and contribution.[27]

How the Game Itself Has Changed over Time

Players and teams are not the only factors for consideration. Over the course of time, the Wealth Transfer and Distribution game has become more complicated.[28] Why? There are many reasons—more than I will discuss here—but in my opinion, this complication is the result of American economic growth for the past hundred-plus years, the complexity of tax-collection measures, the resulting efforts by coaches (professional advisors, attorneys, accountants, bankers, and financial planners) to circumvent these tax measures, and the creation of new asset classes. The cumulative effect of these components has made a simple process more difficult and complicated.[29]

In 1900, most people didn't have significant assets to distribute, and they certainly didn't face the transfer issues we face today. At best, most people had personal items and whatever they managed to acquire in life—perhaps a piece of property or a bit of money. Excessive wealth was narrowly held and focused on tangible assets, and wealth transfer was easier than it is today.

The twentieth century represented a boom era for the United States. Particularly after World War II, increases in personal income fueled the desire to acquire a family home, and the appeal of suburban living made new housing developments more desirable than life within city cores. Concurrently, business development increased as the need and appetite for services grew. Eventually, service companies that didn't manufacture became more valuable and more numerous than those that did.[30]

Government was not blind to these changes; the social needs made apparent by economic disasters like the Great Depression gave rise to social programs that required constant and ever-increasing funding. This funding was provided by income tax, estate tax, and gift tax receipts that contributed heavily to the growth of government itself.[31]

To counteract the government's effort to levy additional taxes, professional advisors sought to defeat or dilute the government's efforts. Because of this, the Wealth Transfer and Distribution game took on more form (i.e., it was *bounded,* as described above) and became what it is today: a game that can't be avoided by anyone who owns property of almost any kind. Viable assets in more hands made distribution a wealth-transfer tax opportunity for the government. This in turn led to significant efforts to change the playing field.

Finally, asset classes themselves changed; personal assets went beyond the family home, and ownership of stocks and bonds became widespread.[32] Tangible assets were joined by intangible assets. Today, for example, there are digital assets such as user passwords and online accounts, which have value and need to be distributed upon the deaths of their owners.[33] Where the game was simple a hundred years ago, it is anything but that today.[34] As players, however, we have to play the game as it is, not as it was. Today anyone who owns anything must be ready and willing to play the game unless he or she wants to let someone else dictate the outcome.[35]

Modifying the Game

By taking an active role in the game, the player gets to define how the game is played.[36] While there are always rules in place, there is also the potential for a skilled player to affect the game in a personal and sometimes permanent way. The rules of most games are generally seen as fixed and unchanging, but they are sometimes subject to modification because of a particular player's skill set.[37] When Lew Alcindor (now Kareem Abdul-Jabbar) attended UCLA, his extraordinary dunking skills proved to be such an advantage that they were perceived as a threat to the fairness upon which any game depends. So the NCAA outlawed dunking in order to level the playing field.[38] The game was modified to fit a new set of circumstances brought about by a single player. Similarly, years later, the North Carolina Tar Heels excelled at a stalling technique known as the "four-corners offense." The NCAA again reacted to the change, this time by instituting the shot clock to force offensive action.[39] In both cases, rule changes were enacted in order to restore fairness to the game. It is noteworthy that even with the changes, UCLA and North Carolina both continued to win championships.

In our game, there are numerous, equally compelling examples of how one player and a favorable court decision can change the game, its rules, and its outcomes. Let's quickly consider the 1991 Cristofani case, which has significant implications.[40] Maria Cristofani set up a trust designed to benefit a small number of immediate beneficiaries—her children—but used a much larger class of secondary beneficiaries—her grandchildren—to supplement her gifting capacity. Maria had three children who stood to gain immediate benefit. With today's annual gifting limits of $14,000, this would create an immediate initial gift of $42,000. However, because the likelihood of the grandchildren benefiting from the trust was small, Maria stretched the rules and included her grandchildren as a remote, secondary class of beneficiaries. By doing this, she created $140,000 in extra annual gifting capacity ($14,000 per ten grandchildren). This raised her gifting allowance from $42,000 to $182,000 per year, and after ten years Maria Cristofani would transfer $1.4 million more than she could have otherwise.

The Cristofani family was scoring a lot of points that Congress and the IRS never intended for anyone to be able to score. Although the IRS fought this action in court for years, the courts ruled in favor of the family and thus made possible a level of gifting that had never existed before. In effect, the Cristofani case had a slam-dunk, four-corners effect on gifting. This illustrates the value of understanding how to play the game.

To be clear, the game of Wealth Transfer and Distribution is not ill defined; it is, however, subject to change by players who challenge its assumptions— i.e., its rules. Rules are as mutable as the roles the players can play.[41] To play the game well, the player must understand what the rules are, how they are enforced through regulations, and most important, how they are likely to change over time.[42] Bigger, smarter, faster, stronger players affect the game. Consequently, concurrent changes are made to the rules of the game in order to try to keep pace with the evolution of the players. Old strategies and tactics can work, but the only way to keep up with the game is to understand the newest positions and anticipate future trends.

The IRS—a Partisan Referee

Almost every game calls for opponents, and the game of Wealth Transfer and Distribution is no different. As with most games, there are multiple opponents; even the rules serve as an opponent of sorts, as do their enforcers.[43]

Most games are not self-regulating. There are moments of self-regulation in sports—for example, a tennis player who calls a foot fault on herself, or a golfer who takes a penalty stroke for grounding his club in a hazard. These are exceptions, however; most of the time, whether we like to admit it or not, we play against not only an opponent, but also the umpire who calls the game. Based on more examples than one could ever give, the player seldom views the umpire as impartial.

In the game of Wealth Transfer and Distribution, there are a multitude of opponents, including those who create the rules and those who apply them, and even the economic, political, or familial environment in which we play. The game is rife with antagonistic forces that need to be identified and addressed.[44]

As a result, this game—which affects almost anyone who owns something of value—requires a time-consuming degree of attention. To play this game well by oneself is nearly impossible. There is too much to know and anticipate, and too many things that need to be done properly for a lone player to be truly successful in most cases. Thus, while it is unusual, but possible, to be successful without the help of others, success is more likely with the assistance of others.[45] (As in sports, however, there are exceptions. Jim Furyk is a great example of a successful golfer whose swing defies coaching; however, even he acknowledges his uniqueness).

Unlike in sports, changes to the rules and regulations governing wealth transfer and distribution are not always publicly or clearly announced. To the contrary, changes often occur as a result of remote court cases or sparsely reported legislative actions of which the player may not be aware. To stay current requires time and effort. Obviously, most players would prefer to just play the game rather than devote endless hours and days to becoming experts on its rules. It is therefore not unusual for successful players to seek out interpreters to help them when necessary ... but otherwise to be silent while the participants play the game.

Professional golf offers a great example of this; it provides rules interpreters to the players on the course so that when questions occur, neutral third parties can make judgments immediately. If a golfer hits a ball into a construction zone and he's not sure whether an object in his way is manmade or part of the course, there is a rules official to whom he can turn for guidance. The golfer's next action will be predicated on the official's ruling.

Similarly, in our wealth transfer game, circumstances may arise in which the rules and regulations are not immediately evident; indeed, they may be quite obscure.[46] In many cases, the only way you could even know that an opportunity or a problem existed would be to ask about it. A case in point: Until April 30, 2016, married couples were able to manipulate their Social Security payments favorably by means of a practice known as "file and suspend."[47] But on May 1, that opportunity vanished, and anyone attempting this manipulation was now in violation of the law. Under normal circumstances, how would anyone know that? In my opinion, unless someone is dedicated to becoming a rules expert, the most reliable way to keep abreast of such changes is to go out and seek the assistance of qualified financial professionals.

Thankfully, despite its complexity and propensity for change, the game of Wealth Transfer and Distribution doesn't require daily attention for most players—and in some cases, not even annual attention—provided they have the assistance they need in order to play it properly. So long as initial decisions are properly made and executed, there is a strong chance that the player can take some time off to play a little defense. Whether on offense or defense, players must ensure that they get the rest they need to play effectively. Ideally, this time away from the game also serves to shorten it. The offense gets to rest while the defense (i.e., the player's team of financial professionals, a subject to be discussed in chapter 4) is on the field protecting the advantages already secured.[48] There are two purposes to rest: shortening the game and protecting the existing advantage. So long as these goals are met, the player can collect himself and renew his supply of energy. However, no player can ever be completely at rest until he or she is completely out of the game.[49]

The Game May Never End

Another key feature of the game is the fact that it is potentially never-ending, and yet the roles that players assume may change. Likewise, the rules governing the game may change, and the assets in play may change as well. In other words, the game of Wealth Transfer and Distribution is dynamic. This is one of the most critical issues for every player to understand. The game is over only when the desired transfer or distribution is complete, when there are no more assets available for transfer or distribution, and when the player has no actions left to take. A case in point would be a player who decides to give away all his or her earthly possessions today and enter a monastery or convent.[50] In this case, the player has effectively retired from the game. While this may have happened more frequently several hundred years ago, modern-day Buddhas or Francises of Assisi are rare! The point here is that the Wealth Transfer and Distribution game doesn't end until the player is dead (or void of assets), her wishes observed, and her assets finally distributed.[51]

Because of the potential length of the game, the role the player fills can change over time. A player can begin as an owner and end up a retired dependent, much like a baseball player who goes from being a starting pitcher to a relief pitcher to a pitching coach to a manager, and finally into retirement. Each time a change occurs, the player is exposed to a different part of the game, and his success is measured by different standards.

Unless one takes action to halt one's participation by giving it all away or dying, the game can be a lifelong pursuit. I have client families who have been playing the game for seventy years and will continue to do so at least until they pass away . . . and there is a strong likelihood in some cases that they will continue to influence the game in absentia through measures that they have imposed on their successors. For this reason, the game of Wealth Transfer and Distribution requires as much diligence after thirty years as it does on day one, and sometimes more. Thus, pacing is important. For many players, the game is a marathon, not a sprint. It requires intellectual appreciation, simple observation, and the ability to be constant in effort and flexible in energy. In the end, the game is what the player chooses for it to be; it can be complicated or easy, quick or long, clean or dirty, but one thing is clear: The game will be played with or without you, whether for one day or for seventy years.[52]

Notes

1. For a great overview to the problems and questions on money, see Sarah Newcomb, 2006, *Loaded: Money, Psychology, and How to Get Ahead without Leaving Your Values Behind*, Hoboken, NJ, John Wiley & Sons Inc. To better understand the downside of the problems discussed here—too little money—see George Schneider, "Woefully Underfunded Retirees Need a Plan: Here's One Solution," *Seeking Alpha*, July 16, 2016. For people with too much money, see Robert G. Kuchner, "When Is an Inheritance Too Big?" *Private Wealth Magazine*, Summer 2016, pages 49–50.
2. If you need an incentive, do the patriotic thing and follow our Founding Fathers in their thinking: Megan Leonhardt and David Lenok, "Independent Legacies: Wills of Our Founding Fathers," *Wealth Management.com*, June 30, 2016.
3. Lawrence Frolik and Bernard A. Krooks. "16 Topics to Discuss at an Initial Client Meeting," *Wealth Management.com*, July 8, 2016. Also see Lance Roberts, "Retirees May Have a Spend Down Problem," *Advisor Perspectives*, July 12, 2016. After years of accumulation, moving to depletion requires careful consideration and evaluation. Failure to plan carefully can lead to financial discomfort and potential ruin.
4. See John Mauldin, "Generational Chaos Ahead," *Thoughts from the Frontline*, June 19, 2016. This article discusses Neil Howe's ideas on how each generation views its economic

fortunes and thus makes its own economic history. For a philosophical approach, see Patricia Angus, "Are You 'Wealthy'?" *Trusts & Estates*, June 30, 2016.

5. Roland McMillan, "What Board Games Can Teach Your Clients About Wealth Management," *Trust Advisor*, April 1, 2016. Catan is a board game, similar to Monopoly, but enhanced by considerations like location, relationships, and use of resources. On an even more basic level, see Glenn Kurlander, *Opening Pandora's Box*, Morgan Stanley, 2013, and "UBS Urges Families to Break the Silence on Inheritance," *Trust Advisor*, July 24, 2014.

6. Annie Lowrey, "What Comes After Rich Baby Boomers? Kids with a Big Inheritance," *New York Times Magazine*, March 11, 2014. This article describes how as much as 35 percent of all US wealth is owned by the top 1 percent. Despite this concentration of wealth, there is significant wealth remaining in the other 99 percent. For how advisors regard millennials, see another point of view: Joanne Cleaver, "How Financial Advisors Are Courting Millennials," *US News*, December 30, 2014.

7. Chuck Rubin, "Sumner Redstone v. Commissioner Assessed 41 Years after Gift," *Steve Leimberg's Estate Planning Newsletter*, February 4, 2016. Care needs to be given to transfers at all times; failure to properly account for transfers can lead to disastrous results even forty years later!

8. In the United States there are three potential types of taxation: income, gift, and estate. When a player transfers assets, any one of these taxes can be imposed, and possibly more than one. In addition, it is necessary to understand that a transfer can occur today while the distribution occurs at a later date. However, the opposite is rarely seen; it is unusual to have a distribution occur with a delayed taxable event. For a great visual overview of income tax history, see Ben Steverman and Dorthy Gambrell, "Never a Convenient time for Childbirth, Death, Or . . . ," *Business Week*, April 11, 2016, pages 24–25.

9. Transfers and their taxes are not always complete when tax is imposed. See "IRS Backs Down on $2.5 Billion of Billionaire Bill Davidson's Estate Tax," *Trust Advisor*, July 12, 2015.

10. For a brief explanation of the application of estate taxes in the United States, see "Policy Basics: The Estate Tax," Center on Budget and Policy Priorities, July 5, 2016.

11. It is refreshing to see someone play the game well. Athletes historically have wasted wealth; however, a recent example of success warrants mention. Scott Martin, "Did Muhammad Ali Leave the Greatest $50 Million Estate Plan of All Time?" *Trust Advisor*, June 6, 2016.

12. The size of the transfer is disputed. For two differing opinions, see Ansuya Harjani, "The Biggest Family Wealth Transfers in History Are About to Happen," CNBC, October 13, 2015, and Mamta Badkar, "We're on the Verge of the Greatest Transfer of Wealth in the History of the World," *Business Insider*, June 12, 2014. For long-term consumption patterns, see Eric Bush, "The Long View of US Income and Consumption Patterns," *Advisor Perspectives*, February 1, 2016. For numbers of employees with retirement accounts, see *Position Your Business for Success in The New Retirement Reality*, Pershing LLC, June 2016.

13. To see what's at stake, review RBC Wealth Management's report, "Until Death Do Us Part . . . Then Everything Can Change" and "The Golden Rule of Estate Planning: Your Spouse Comes First," *Trust Advisor*, May 7, 2015.

14. Nancy Mann Jackson, "The Five Rules of Personal Finance That Everyone Should Memorize," *The Muse*, May 2015.

15. David H. Lenok, "Wealthiest Plan Investors Are Least Satisfied, Most Pessimistic," *Wealth Management.Com*, May 27, 2016; Jerry Wagner, "Investing Without a Goal is Like Racing Without a Finish Line,"*Advisor Perspectives*, May 28, 2015.

16. Incompatibility Can Cost You," *Trust Advisor*, June 4, 2015. For an interesting look at neglect in planning, see Jacob Shamsian, "Snoop Dogg Told Us Why He Doesn't Have a Will," *Business Insider*, May 5, 2016. Also see Vanessa McGrady, "Facebook's Advice to

Advisors: Here's What 70 Million Millennials Want," *Forbes*, February 3, 2016, and Andrew Bloomenthal, "The New Trend for Millennial Investors," CNBC, February 19, 2016.

17. For a simple introduction to business valuation, see "Business Valuation Methods," *SME Toolkit*; for real estate, see Arthur Pinkasovitch, "How to Value a Real Estate Investment Property," *Investopedia*.

18. Peter Brooks, Greg Davies, Robert Smith, "A Behavioral Perspective on Goal-Based Investing," *Advisor Perspectives*, May 12, 2016. Special care needs to be given to families with noncitizen spouses. Given recent trends in immigration, this is a growing issue that rarely gets the attention it deserves. See Jennifer J. Wioncek, "Limitations on the Use of the Unlimited Marital Deduction for Non-Citizen Spouses and Practical Alternatives," *Steve Leimberg's International Tax Planning Newsletter*, April 12, 2016.

19. David Lansky, "Time and Tide: The Legacy Dream," *Private Wealth Magazine*, Summer 2016, pages 13, 57.

20. Celebrities provide excellent examples of what to do and what not to do in transfer and distribution planning. For tales of recent success (and failure), see the following: Scott Martin, "Robin Williams, Joan Rivers, Philip Seymour Hoffman: Why Some Stars Left More Durable Legacies," *Trust Advisor*, December 14, 2014; Megan Elliott, "7 Tips on Planning Your Estate, from the Mistakes of Celebrities," *Cheat Sheet*, October 6, 2015. Also see Bruce Steiner, "Lessons from Prince's Lack of a Will," *Steve Leimberg's Estate Planning Email Newsletter*, June 7, 2016, and Stacy E. Singer, "When Doves Cry—and the Tax Man Chuckles," *Trusts & Estates*, May 6, 2016.

21. Sarah Newcomb, "How to Manage Wealth Across Generations," *Trust Advisor*, September 29, 2015. Another key issue for consideration is whether women have unique planning needs; see: Andrea Coombes, "Women & Estate Planning: Universal or Unique Challenges?" *Marketwatch*, May 9, 2014. This can be especially important given that women currently are estimated to control 51 percent of the wealth in the United States; see Steve Garmhausen, "Out of the Shadows," *Barron's*, June 6, 2016, S18.

22. Lacey Kessler, "This Estate Mistake Can Tear Your Family Apart," *Trust Advisor*, March 21, 2016. Another interesting issue concerns pets: Keith Schiller, "Ted 2 Inspires Analysis of Administrative Expense Deductions for Pre-distribution Pet Care," *Steve Leimberg's Estate Planning E-mail Newsletter*, November 10, 2015.

23. Deborah Ermann and Nicole Shrive, "Preparing Children for Wealth," *Premier Trust*, April 2014.

24. Gregory Curtis, "Family-Centric Portfolios," *Private Wealth*, March 2014.

25. Mohamed A. El-Erian, "Unburdening the Facebook Generation," *Project Syndicate*, July 18, 2016. For a negative view of retirement prospects, see Gary D. Halbert, *Forecasts & Trends E-Letter*, May 17, 2016.

26. The blended family presents even more challenges over the traditional family; see "Estate Planning for Blended Families," *Premier Trust*, June 2016.

27. Sarah Newcomb, "Financial Turning Points: The Parent's Dilemma," *Morningstar Behavioral Finance for Advisors*, July 18, 2016. Also see Steven Maimes, "High-Net-Worth Families Add Complexity to Wealth Management," *Trust Advisor*, June 5, 2015.

28. See Patricia M. Soldano, "How 2016 Election May Affect Estate Planning," *Trusts & Estates*, June 10, 2016. Similarly, tax changes are seen to be helpful; see John Tamny, "How the Risks of the Wealthy Help the Middle Class," *Reason*, March 11, 2016.

29. Richard Michaud, "Financing Education is a Retirement Issue," *Advisor Perspectives*, May 20, 2016.

30. For a brief overview, see "Economic History of the United States," *Wikipedia*, sections 6–10.

31. Bryan D. Kirk, "Greenbooks in Spring," *Trusts & Estates*, May 10, 2016. Despite all the economic advances, economic disparity continued to grow throughout the last half of the

twentieth century. For more, see this article originating from the Federal Reserve Bank of St. Louis: Ray Boshara, "Thrivers and Strugglers: A Growing Economic Divide," *Econintersect*.

32. Tangible assets took even broader forms: Roland McMillan, "Guidance on Protecting Family, Sperm, Eggs, and Embryos," Trust Advisor, June 22, 2016. Also see David Shayne, "Benefits Due a Child Conceived After a Parent's Death," Steve Leimberg's Estate Planning Newsletter, February 24, 2016; Jennifer Kelly, "Trust Fund Babies: The Pros and Cons of Trusts for Newborns," Trust Advisor, April 21, 2014; and Darren M. Wallace and Laura A. Schuyler, "Potential Intellectual Property Issues Emerge for Prince's Estate," Trusts & Estates, April 26, 2016.

33. Roland McMillan, "The Full Potential of Wealth Management," Trust Advisor, February 22, 2016; also see Steve Cook, "Facebook's Tool for Your Digital Estate Plan," Trust Advisor, May 15, 2015, and Suzanne Brown Walsh, "The Status of the Uniform Fiduciary Access to Digital Assets Act," Steve Leimberg's Estate Planning Newsletter, April 9, 2015.

34. Sarah Newcomb, "'How to Manage Wealth Across Generations," Trust Advisor, September 29, 2015.

35. To see how things are changing, see Michael Raneri, "7 Ways Wealth Management Client Attitudes Are Shifting," Trust Advisor, May 14, 2015, and Joanne Cleaver, "How Boomers Are Redefining 'Legacy'," US News, July 8, 2015.

36. Richard Bernstein, "Taking Grounders in Spring Training," Advisor Perspectives, November 12, 2015.

37. Similarly, changes can be imposed when circumstances require additional help or support. See Lacey Kessler, "Trust Company to Temporarily Manage Prince's Estate," Trust Advisor, May 23, 2016.

38. For a brief overview of the "Lew Alcindor rule," see "Slam Dunk," Wikipedia; dunking in college basketball was outlawed from 1967–1976.

39. "Four Corners Offense—Complete Coaching Guide," Basketball for Coaches, April 11, 2016.

40. For a brief summary of the Cristofani case, see "Estate of Cristofani v. Commissioner," Case Briefs, http://www.casebriefs.com/blog/law/wills-trusts-estates/wills-trusts-estates-keyed-to-dukeminier/wealth-transfer-taxation-tax-planning/estate-of-cristofani-v-commissioner/.

41. For a tabular chart of changes in estate tax rates and lifetime exemptions since 2002, see "Policy Basics: The Estate Tax," Center on Budget and Policy Priorities, July 5, 2016.

42. Conrad Teitell, "House Bill to Authorize Charitable Life-Income IRA Rollovers," Wealth Management, May 6, 2016.

43. In some cases, legislative results come to favor one group of taxpayers over another; see Barbara Roper, "Middle-Income Savers Big Winners from DOL Conflict Rule," Wealth Management.com, May 3, 2016. Also see Lacey Kessler, "Can Naysayers Kill DOL Fiduciary Rule?" Trust Advisor, May 3, 2016.

44. For IRS squabbles, see Kevin Packman, "Windfall from Abroad Brings Home IRS Compliance Issues," Steve Leimberg's International Tax Planning Email Newsletter, May 5, 2016. For family squabbles, see Scott Martin, "Frank Zappa Trust Cuts Heirs Out of $40 Million Family Name," Trust Advisor, May 19, 2016. For societal squabbles, see John Mauldin, "Life on the Edge," Mauldin Economics, May 14, 2016.

45. If you doubt the wisdom of "going it alone," find support here: Robert Holton, "How to Give Away a Billion Dollar Jackpot," Wealth Management.com, February 5, 2016. For a more practical example, see Robert E. Sharpe Jr., "A Golden Age for Real Estate Gifts," Wealth Management.com, February 19, 2016.

46. An example of opaque tax legislation is the Consolidated Appropriations Act, HR 2029, passed in December 2015.

47. See the Social Security Administration's website for more information about file and suspend: https://www.ssa.gov/planners/retire/suspend.html.

48. Nothing is more deflating than having an issue arise with the IRS years after you thought it had been settled: Chuck Rubin, "Sumner Redstone v. Commissioner: Gift Taxes Assessed 41 Years after Gift," Steve Leimberg's Estate Planning Email Newsletter, February 4, 2016.

49. In some cases, the resolution of a person's distribution/transfer wishes can take years, even after death. The Tax Code offers at least two ways to extend the payment of transfer taxes: code sections 6161 and 6166. Special care should be given when using either of these options since failure to comply with expected payments can have severe consequences; see "By the Grace of . . . ," McGuire Woods Consulting, October 17, 2013.

50. There are several examples of people making strong commitments to endow the world, including Warren Buffet, Bills Gates, and others. However, there are lesser-known individuals equally committed to incredible charity; see Tavia Grant, "Meet the Canadian Billionaire Who's Giving It All Away," The Globe and Mail, May 26, 2012.

51. This is also known as the settlement process, and things do go wrong; see "James Brown Estate Settlement Overturned in South Carolina," Rolling Stone, February 28, 2013.

52. Longevity is a growing issue today in the United States. Plainly stated, we live longer than our bodies naturally can support us and at costs that were never anticipated, even twenty years ago. See Carol Einhorn, "What Every Professional Should Know about LTCI in 2016," Steve Leimberg's Elder Care Law Planning Newsletter, March 3, 2016; Rodney L. Goodwin, "Medicaid Qualified Annuities and Costs of Long Term Care," Wealth Management.com, July 5, 2016; John M Goralka, "Estate Planning for an Aging Population," Trust & Estates, July 5, 2016; "New Longevity Will Cause Financial Advisors to Change How They Give Advice," Trust Advisor, October 20, 2015.

Chapter 3

Understanding the Rules

———————◆———————

Prologue

The regulations governing the game of Wealth Transfer and Distribution are often ill-defined and always subject to change. Despite this, the game can be rewarding if you understand the rules. Most of the steps taken by the couple in the material below have income-, gift-, or estate-tax implications.

Connie had an adult son, Rex, who had Asperger's syndrome and was unable to support himself without assistance.[1] Since Connie knew that Rex's future was at risk, she looked for ways to assist him. Happily, she had economic means, and her husband, Chuck, was willing to help financially even though Rex was not his son.

Connie studied the Tax Code, and found that it imposes a gift tax of up to 40 percent on gifts in excess of $14,000 in any year. Since Rex's needs far exceeded $14,000 in any given year, Connie needed to learn how to use the system to her advantage. As her first modification, she convinced Chuck to *gift-split* with her; by making another $14,000 gift to Rex in Chuck's name, Connie doubled her gifting capacity.

Second, Rex needed training to become more employable, and Connie discovered a way to offset the cost of this as well—by making all tuition payments directly to the school on Rex's behalf. She used the same approach when it came to medical costs; by making payments directly to the doctor or hospital, she expanded her gifting capacity beyond the $14,000-per-person rule.

Next, they agreed that Chuck should employ Rex in his business, which would enable Chuck to assist Rex without creating another gift. Chuck paid Rex $25,000 a year, which created a downstream benefit for Rex because while working, he would accumulate the credits necessary to receive Social Security payments and Medicare benefits later in life. Since $25,000 was a modest salary, Rex faced little in the way of income taxes. Thus, the money he earned was money he kept.

Housing was a potential long-term issue for Rex. Given his low earning capacity, he was unlikely ever to purchase property on his own. Renting was not a good long-term solution because rents were likely to increase over time and could potentially exceed Rex's ability to afford them. For this reason, Connie and Chuck decided to buy a modest condo for Rex—and found that the mortgage payment was lower than comparable rental costs.

However, this solution entailed its own problems. In the eyes of the IRS, Connie and Chuck had made another gift in the form of rent-free living, and by doing so, they had now exceeded their annual gifting allowance because the rent they didn't receive amounted to $1,000 in additional gifts per month, and that amount would likely increase over time as comparable rents increased.

Fortunately, Connie and Chuck had another gifting option—the Lifetime Exemption. This exemption gave each of them a free money allowance of around $5.5 million that could be used in life or at death to shelter gifts from tax. After they agreed once again to split gifts, they each filed a gift-tax return for amounts exceeding $14,000; this filing used a very small portion of their large exemption. While it took some time to complete the gift-tax return, they incurred no direct tax cost as a result of their gift.

Through these actions, Connie helped Rex live a more independent life. She had a final concern, however: What would happen when she died? Since Rex was not Chuck's son, Connie wanted to be sure that when she passed, nothing would encumber Chuck or undermine her efforts to provide for Rex.

To ensure Rex's future, Connie took two more steps. She created a tax-free cash reserve for Rex and worked with Chuck to transfer ownership interest in the condo to Rex. The first step resulted in a trust funded with life insurance. By making modest annual gifts, Connie and Chuck created a warehouse of ready funds that Rex could access upon Connie's death.

Tax-advantaged treatment is a benefit of owning life insurance. Under normal circumstances, life insurance proceeds carry no income tax liability. However, by establishing a special trust designed to hold life insurance, Connie used another section of tax law favorably. When she and Chuck made annual contributions to this trust, a special provision tax-qualified the funds and allowed them to buy life insurance without triggering either gift- or estate-tax treatment on the death benefits. They gave Rex short-term withdrawal rights every time funds were advanced. By giving him a thirty-day withdrawal period, the trust offered him access to the funds; once the thirty-day period elapsed without him withdrawing funds, the trust could apply the money to life insurance. Through this technique, Connie made sure that Rex would have a lump sum available when she passed. This planning approach met two family goals: It enriched Rex, and it obviated the need for Chuck to support Rex after Connie died.

Connie and Chuck agreed to pass the condo's ownership directly to Rex at Connie's death, and Connie made this provision in her estate documents. Knowing that Rex would have both guaranteed funds and a home when his mother died eased her mind considerably.

To realize her objectives, Connie needed to work with both Chuck and Rex, and she needed to understand how she could use various planning approaches. By understanding the rules and regulations, Connie and Chuck made sure that they delivered every possible benefit at the lowest tax costs. Their efforts took planning, but the end results created the life Connie wanted for Rex and minimized her tax costs.

The Law Is the Law Is the Law . . . Except When It Isn't

Almost all games have rules, and many games are subject to rules that change over time. Even in those few games whose rules don't change, the *interpretation* of those rules changes over time, which in turn changes how the rules are applied.

It is no different in the game of Wealth Transfer and Distribution. Our court system is one of the primary sources of rule changes, as can be seen in the decisions made by the Circuit Courts of Appeal.

In the United States there are thirteen Circuit Courts of Appeal. In accordance with human nature, there is clear evidence that when judging particular kinds of cases, certain circuits traditionally view taxpayer issues more favorably than others. As a result, it is common for attorneys to bring cases before specific Courts of Appeal in hopes of securing their desired outcomes.[2] This may be seen as analogous to the variation we see among umpires in baseball: Although the strike zone is a constant—it is the area directly over the plate, extending vertically from the batter's knees to the midpoint of his torso—some subjectivity creeps into the calling of pitches that reach the edges of this zone. This means that some umpires have a broader—one might say, a more liberal—perception of the strike zone than others, and are therefore more likely to call a questionable pitch a strike. Some umpires can therefore be said to be more liberal or more conservative than their counterparts in their application of their understanding of the rules.

It is no different in the game of Wealth Transfer and Distribution. Outcomes often differ depending upon who makes the call. In our game, there are rules, there are regulations, and there are interpreters. Depending on the facts and circumstances, how the player and his team are affected by the application of the rules depends on who is officiating the game. This is one reason why the game of Wealth Transfer and Distribution requires a clear understanding of the rules and regulations (legislation), how they change over time (modification), and how they are applied (interpretation). Just as each individual umpire has his own perception of the strike zone, every judge interprets tax law differently in one way or another. This, then, requires of us a clear understanding of what is expected from one game to another.

One would think that federal and state tax codes could be applied consistently and fairly, and that court decisions would follow the same logic from case to case. Surely, laws and regulations written down and laid out in black and white should provide dependable guidance to all players and umpires. In reality, the opposite is often true. In many cases, trying to understand the regulations and their applications while playing the Wealth Transfer and Distribution game is a bit like being Alice in Wonderland; the expected is wrong while the unexpected is right.

Discouraging as it may be to learn how susceptible the law can be to judicial whims, there is a positive side to its elasticity: When the player learns the rules and applies them for her own benefit, the playing field can be tilted in the same way that we can tilt a pinball machine to make the ball go where we want it to go.

To return to our baseball analogy, while it is easy to accept a called strike, it is also possible to dispute the call and win. Many sports today allow replays, which make it possible for the on-field manager or players to protest a call and subject the ruling to review and potential reversal. The same thing is true in our game. By understanding the rules, it is possible to change the initial decision to an outcome more to the team's liking. We can challenge an initial IRS determination by making use of the IRS's appeal process. We can seek to overturn bad laws by challenging them in court, or we can lobby our representatives and senators to alter the law. However, doing this requires time, money, patience, conviction, and a firm grasp of the rules.[3]

The Constant Fine-Tuning of the Rules

A basic understanding of the rules and regulations is necessary if you want to enable your team to use the rules to your benefit.[4] To achieve this understanding, it is important to realize that these rules are ever-changing.[5] Throughout our lives we are led to believe that the law is set in stone, but in reality, it is written in chalk . . . and there are always plenty of erasers to go around.[6]

For example, consider how easily you can make a right turn on a red light when driving. In many western states—most notably California—this perfectly safe maneuver has been permitted for over half a century. But this wasn't always the case, as some readers may be old enough to remember. The right-turn-on-red rule began to catch on in eastern states in the early

1970s, and by 1978, it was the law in all fifty states. In the intervening years, however, the inconsistent application of this rule from one state to another caused confusion and occasional anxiety for many interstate drivers: *I've never been to Hawaii before; can I make a right on red here? Other drivers behind me are honking their horns, so maybe I should go . . . but there's a cop in the next lane! I don't want to get a ticket.* What to do? (For many people, driving is a game!)

Form vs. Substance

Running alongside the changing nature of the rules and regulations is the player's constant desire to fine-tune the game. Most of the time this fine-tuning occurs as a result of teams finding ways to create advantages for themselves. For example, recall our discussion in the previous chapter of North Carolina's Tar Heels and their stalling tactic, the "four-corners offense." The four-corners offense worked thus: Four players would stand at the corners of the offensive half-court while the fifth just stood in the middle dribbling the ball until the clock ran out. This tactic would enable the team to hold onto its lead, and it was well within the rules of the game . . . and completely contrary to the spirit of those rules. Not only did the four-corners offense make athleticism irrelevant; it was also considered unsportsmanlike, and boring for spectators.

To negate what it deemed to be a misuse of the rules, the NCAA instituted a shot clock specifically to stamp out this practice. This change revolutionized college basketball by leveling the playing field and giving teams the opportunity to snatch victory from the jaws of defeat. In effect, this change took a nearly guaranteed win away from North Carolina and any other team that chose to minimize scoring in the last few minutes of the game by freezing the ball.

The same kinds of changes are often made to the regulations governing wealth transfer and distribution, and for the same reasons. There is an inherent conflict between the rule makers and the teams, which seems to obligate those who make the rules to adjust them in order to reduce the likelihood of guaranteed outcomes for the teams. Obviously, it was frustrating for Tar Heels players and fans to see their team "punished" for playing within the rules, but the NCAA had a larger issue in mind; its concern was for the game as a whole. While the four-corners offense was within the letter of the law, it offended the spirit of the game.

Along the same lines, the IRS, the leading interpreter and applier of rules in our game, has the ability to argue its position in two ways: *form over substance* and *substance over form*. This means the IRS can take a position in one case that focuses on the spirit of the game (substance over form), and at the same time, argue for the letter of the law in another (form over substance) . . . which fosters the Alice in Wonderland environment I described earlier.7 When red can be white—and white, red—which is right?

For this reason, guaranteed outcomes in the Wealth Transfer and Distribution game are sometimes hard to find. The IRS *occasionally* provides clarity and surety, but in most cases, when it comes to rules and their applications, the team must hold their collective breath while the final decision is being made.8

Further complicating the issue of rules and regulations is the presumption that the player or the team bears the burden of proof. The clearest evidence of this is the need to argue your case. When a controversial call is made in almost any sport, one team is generally the aggrieved party and takes the position of issuing a complaint. In the case of Wealth Transfer and Distribution, we have a less-than-level playing field when it comes to the application of rules or regulations. In our game, those applying the rules and passing judgment are often our opponents rather than neutral third parties. In a game in which your opponent can call foul without the burden of proof, the situation changes from one in which you contend you are right to one in which you must prove you aren't wrong. It is not enough to be right; it is necessary to *show* that your opponent's position is wrong.[9] In the Wealth Transfer and Distribution game, the opposition is both playing against you and officiating the game.

No Guarantees

So how do we learn all the rules and regulations? How do we come to understand the probability of acceptable rulings? Is there a way to determine ahead of time the likelihood of a successful protest? More important, is it possible to set the stage in such a way that our desired outcome is more likely than not? What are the sources of rules and regulations in the game of Wealth Transfer and Distribution?

The rules come from various sources: legislative action, court cases, IRS and state tax proclamations, letter rulings, Department of Labor rules and regulations, and culturally accepted practices. All these sources come together to form the full set of what I am calling "rules and regulations."[10] Needless to say, it would be difficult for any individual to come to grips with all these components, even in a static environment—and these sources are dynamic and changing. Moreover, they can be unclear and even contradictory. So, for the player and his team to come to an understanding of the rules and regulations is very difficult. Happily, there is help. Just as an athletic team depends on its coaches, the Wealth Transfer and Distribution team has its coaching staff— different coaches whose varied expertise enables the manager, the player, and the team to play the game to the best of their collective ability (we will learn more about teams and team building in chapter 5).

Playing to the best of a team's ability, however, doesn't guarantee success. One of the most frustrating and rewarding aspects of any game is the lack of guarantees. But this should not discourage anyone from playing. Quite to the contrary—unlike sporting events in which the outcomes are truly dependent on how the game is played, our game allows the team and players to set the table more securely and to build in a likelihood of success far greater than what would be possible in a typical sporting event.

When we play almost any sport, the outcome is always in question. Even in contests that appear to be grossly unequal, upsets occur—expected easy victories that turn into unbelievable losses. Indeed, the unpredictability of these events is a primary reason for our interest in sports. Although we expect victory, we don't light our victory cigar until the game is over. Even when the end of the game seems to have come clearly into view, we can be surprised; consider the 2015 Super Bowl, when the Seattle Seahawks were on the verge of an inspiring come-from-behind victory. After struggling early in the season, the team rallied and won nine of its last ten regular-season games. Flush with these victories, the Seahawks stormed into the Super Bowl, ending the third quarter with a ten-point lead . . . only to throw away the game in the last quarter. Miracle wins and losses happen in sports.

If these were the conditions under which our Wealth Transfer and Distribution game were played, it would be much less appealing. In our game, players generally look for the closest thing to a guaranteed outcome. Frankly, we want to minimize risk in our game. We aren't putting in all this time and effort only to see victory taken from us at the last moment.

Playing the Game to Its Conclusion

Despite their best efforts to minimize risk, players sometimes lose when they think they should win. In many cases, these losses occur not because of what the IRS does, but because the player fails to play the game to its logical conclusion. There are court cases galore that show players well on the way to victory, only to snatch defeat from the jaws of victory. Why does this happen? Usually because too little attention has been paid to the rules and regulations that limit or define the players' actions. In other words, the team loses because it defeats itself.[11]

As far as I am concerned, this is the primary reason why knowing, understanding, and correctly interpreting the rules and regulations is so important in the Wealth Transfer and Distribution game. Knowing what you can do safely and where the danger lies makes all the difference in the world when it comes to results. By *knowing* the rules and regulations, players can reduce the likelihood of making fatal mistakes. By *understanding* the rules and regulations, the team and player position themselves in the best way to play the game. Finally, when it comes to *interpreting* the rules and regulations, players need to understand that this is where the potential exists to reap the greatest benefit—or inflict the greatest harm. No matter how good the team, failure to properly appreciate how the rules and regulations affect the game can be catastrophic. A lesser team with a greater understanding of the rules has an advantage over a stronger team limited by ignorance or hubris.

An example here might help: Twenty years ago I had a client, Jim, who was in the process of selling his privately owned company to a publicly traded company for an amount of money that carried significant capital gains tax exposure. In discussing the sale with him, I learned that he was happy with the deal in general but unhappy with the potential tax impact of the transaction. I asked Jim if he or his advisors had considered a stock-for-stock sale to minimize the impact. He confessed that he didn't know what this was or how it worked. I explained that this technique allows the owner of stock to trade or exchange his stock for the stock in another company without creating a taxable event, and that this would serve to defer his taxes to a later date. He replied that I had to be wrong because if this option existed, either his advisors or those of the acquiring company would have mentioned it to him!

I begged him to at least approach his advisors for comment, and on the following Monday, he called to tell me that I was right. When I asked why no one else had brought this option to his attention, he replied that they hadn't thought the tax burden was big enough to be important to him. In fact, the tax burden had been the principal obstacle to the deal. With this suggestion, Jim had the solution in hand that would allow him to move forward and close the deal.

But what if he hadn't taken my advice? Or what if he hadn't been my client in the first place? His stubbornness and his lack of curiosity might have cost him that deal. His advisors' laziness and his own unwillingness to pursue a potentially profitable line of inquiry—remember, I had to *beg* him to ask his other advisors about the stock-for-stock sale option—might have cost him a fortune.[12]

The Hidden Ball Trick

What should be learned from this example? Simply this: As we learn the rules and explore the regulations, we begin to see how they can be used to help the team and the player. Furthermore, this understanding and appreciation allows us to adapt our strategies and tactics to use the rules in ways that were not originally intended.

There are countless applications of creativity in the Wealth Transfer and Distribution game. Both football and baseball have a hidden ball trick, although the benefit of this trick differs in each game. In baseball, the purpose of the hidden-ball trick is to get an out without putting the ball in play. The pitcher throws the ball to the first baseman to keep the opposing team's runner closer to the base. Instead of returning the ball to the pitcher, the first baseman fakes the throw and holds the ball. When the opposing team's player leaves the base, the first baseman tags him out. The result of this deception? The opposing team loses a runner and records an out.

In football, the deception is designed as an offensive maneuver. In this case, the quarterback pretends to hand the ball to a running back, who carries out the fake by running the play just as aggressively as he normally does. Assuming the play is run to the right, the opposing team follows the runner, believing that he has the ball. However, since the quarterback has the ball, he now has two options: running to the left on his own or passing to one of his players in a less defended part of the field. Irrespective of which option the quarterback chooses, the result of this deception is an opportunity for offensive success.

A similar approach is available in our game. By understanding the rules and regulations, it is possible in the game of Wealth Transfer and Distribution to make more look like less. Here's a simple example: A family has a valuable piece of property that it wishes to divide among its children. Since retitling a property isn't always easy, the family contributes this property to a partnership. Because the family wants to be sure that this property stays within the immediate family, it imposes restrictions within the partnership. For example, it states that in case of divorce, interest in the property must stay with family members. The imposition of these restrictions within this partnership obviously creates limitations. These limitations, in turn, serve to make ownership of this asset more complicated. As a result of the placement of the property in a partnership and the imposition of restrictions, the ownership value is decreased. In fact, the property is worth neither more nor less than it was outside the partnership, but the "strings" attached to the partnership are cause for devaluation. As such, when all is said and done, the perceived value of the percentage ownership inside the partnership is 20 percent to 40 percent less than if it were unencumbered.[13]

As can be seen by this example, hiding the ball by placing it inside a partnership delivers significant valuation benefits. The player and team can use this approach as either a defensive measure (it makes sure that this valuable property stays within the family) or an offensive measure (it makes something look less valuable). We will discuss the distinction between offense and defense in later chapters.

Use Those Loopholes while They're Open!

In our game, the makers of rules and regulations are typically slow to react to innovative players' creative interpretations and applications of those rules; that is, there is often lag time between the first unorthodox use of a rule and the time when the loophole is closed. This is a time of opportunity for the alert player, and the team that promotes an active and dynamic understanding of the rules is likely to find applications that can be used to its advantage. In some cases, years pass before changes are made to close a loophole.

This situation played out for years in the life insurance industry, where a premium-sharing technique known as "split dollar" was used to finance benefits for selected key employees, resulting in an approach that amounted to a tax-free, no-interest loan. This technique provided the favored employee with de facto free use of corporate money.

This trick found favor in major public corporations as a way to enrich high-level employees and keep them from moving to competitors. At the same time, while this technique could be used at privately held companies (for the owners, at the very least), it was not used as frequently because coaches (attorneys, accountants, and even financial advisors) were less acquainted with it than they should have been. For those few players who used this approach, it became a way to extract value from the business without stepping out of bounds. Ultimately, congressional legislation narrowed this loophole, but Congress still preserved most of the benefit for employees of companies that had adopted these plans prior to the legislative tightening. By finding gaps in the rules and regulations, major corporations and some private companies made use of a technique that was at odds with normal public policy.

There is an important implicit lesson in this last example: It is not necessary to break the rules to win the game. In many cases, the established limits define how to win the game at the base level. In these cases, the rules and regulations provide the blueprint for success. A current example that supports this point is a technique now being used to gift family vacation homes (cabins, family retreats, extravagant vacation properties) to younger generations at a discount without the parents surrendering control and effective ownership (and use) for a specified number of years. This technique, called a Qualified Personal Residence Trust (or QPRT), is available to anyone whose circumstances allow for it.[14] Without going into detail, when the player and team follow the rules laid out in the Tax Code, this technique entails little risk. By following a rules-and-regulations recipe, the player can deliver an asset to future generations at a discount today while postponing tax on future appreciation. This is not to say that this technique has no drawbacks, but by simply following the rules, the player and team can win.

It is essential for every player to understand that there are opportunities lying at our feet. Once those opportunities are identified, the player and his team must endeavor to see whether there are ways to improve upon them. There is nothing wrong with trying to make a good thing better, so long as we don't get greedy. But the biggest mistake most players make is the failure to understand what they can do in the first place—legally and with controlled risk.

In the game of Wealth Transfer and Distribution, rules and regulations should be viewed as positives, not negatives. Rules and regulations frame the questions; they bound the problems. They are not only limits; they also provide insight into how our opponents think and what those opponents see as issues. At the same time, the rules and regulations are largely reactive to past issues. For this reason, they often fail to address current thinking and application. In other words, the rules by their very nature are outdated almost as soon as they are promulgated. Thus, the player with a good team and good coaches should be looking for soft spots to exploit. In the end, successful players use the rules to direct themselves to even greater opportunities.[15]

Notes

1.   Martin M. Shenkman, Neil D. Blicher, Anthony R. Barlett, and Dania Jekel, "Planning for an Individual with Asperger Syndrome," *Trusts & Estates*, April 2016, pages 14–19. For new legislation designed to assist the disabled, see the Achieving a Better Life Experience (ABLE) Act, passed in 2014.

2. For a fascinating look at how courts can "make law," see Owen Fiore, "Estate of Giustina v. Commissioner," *Steve Leimberg's Estate Planning E-mail Newsletter*, June 27, 2016 and June 28, 2016. In another case, the dissenting judge claimed that his colleagues had performed a miracle by making "nothing out of something." See also Steve Leimberg, "Dorrance v. US: Result in Demutualization Case Reversed," *Steve Leimberg's Income Tax Planning Newsletter*, February 16, 2016.

3. Proposals are often overlooked; there are any number of tax studies going on at any given time. As a result, it is also important and valuable to see what is being considered; see "High Earners Are Going to Hate These Retirement Proposals," *Bloomberg News*, June 9, 2016.

4. The obvious tax bible is *The Tax Code, Regulations and Official Guidance*. However, most people are disinclined to dive into the Code, with good reason. Two publications that lend themselves to greater ease of use are *Tax Facts* (http://pro.nuco.com/Pages/default.aspx) and the *US Master Tax Guide*. Both of these publications are more user-friendly, especially *Tax Facts*, which contains different sections on *Insurance & Employee Benefits*, *Investments*, and *Individuals and Small Business*. These handy references are available both online and on paper. The *US Master Tax Guide* is a little denser, but also a great resource for answers to perplexing problems.

5. To make the point as clear as possible, new rules for advisors to retirement accounts stretch over one thousand pages! See David Armstrong, "The Fine Lines of the Fiduciary Rule," NAPA 401(k) Summit, April 19, 2016.

6. For a sense of how different opinion letters can be, go to http://www.legalbitstream.com/irs_materials.asp?pl=i9, where you can research Private Letter Rulings. See the following: PLR 201628004 overrode court orders that had provided direction on reforming beneficiary designations to allow benefits to be stretched over the lives of beneficiaries. PLR 201627006, on the other hand, granted a waiver of the sixty-day rollover requirement allowing the transfer of qualified retirement funds to an IRA. PLR 201623001 ruled that a surviving spouse was not allowed to roll over her community property interest in an IRA. However, there is no ruling that IRAs can preempt community property claims to death benefits (Michael J. Jones, "PLR 201623001," *Steve Leimberg's Employee Benefits and Retirement Planning Newsletter*, July 6, 2016). States also participate in this process through legislation, and by actively trying to make themselves more attractive to players with planning ambitions; see Kristen Simmons, "SB484: Nevada Legislature Allows for Greater Flexibility with Irrevocable Trusts," *Steve Leimberg's Estate Planning E-mail Newsletter*, June 16, 2015.

7. "What Is Substance over Form?" *Accounting Tools*, http://www.accountingtools.com/questions-and-answers/what-is-substance-over-form.html; also see Tyler Horton, "Substance, Form, and Ambiguity: Will the IRS Challenge Your Transaction by Asserting the Economic Substance Doctrine?" *Alvarez & Marsal*, February 10, 2014, and Joseph B. Darby, "Forms over Substance: IRS Information Reporting Surges," *Tax and Sports Update*, February 26, 2016. Every year we can expect new guidelines for everything from income tax brackets to personal-exemption phase outs to other points deserving our interest; it is critical for every player to understand how much the tax environment changes from year to year. For a short but handy guide, see Blanche Lark Christenson, "Tax Topics," *Deutsche Asset & Wealth Management*, October 26, 2015._

8. Bruce D. Steiner, "New IRS Regulations Benefit IRA Participants," *Trusts & Estates*, May 24, 2016. For cases that still leave questions in the air, see Ron Aucutt, "Woebling: Parties Settle Closely Watched Court Cases Involving Defined Value Clause," *Steve Leimberg's Estate Planning E-mail Newsletter*, May 24, 2016, or J. Alan Jensen and R. Brent Berselli, "Estate of Morrissette: Unfinished Business," *Steve Leimberg's Estate Planning Newsletter*, May 23, 2016. Also see Chuck Rubin, "Costello v. Commissioner: Income Tax Assessment on

Beneficiary Allowed Even Though the Statute of Limitations Had Expired," *Steve Leimberg's Estate Planning E-mail Newsletter*, April 7, 2016.

9. For the IRS position on this issue, see "Burden of Proof," https://www.irs.gov/businesses/small-businesses-self-employed/burden-of-proof, April 25, 2016.

10. Private Letter Rulings or PLRs are one of the more common and readable sources of information on tax issues. However, special care must be given to their use and interpretation, since each ruling applies only to the taxpayer seeking direction. As such, they are not transferable; however, they do serve to provide some insight into current IRS thinking. See "Private Letter Rulings," *Tax Almanac*, http://www.taxalmanac.org/index.php/Private_Letter_Rulings.html.

11. A classic case of snatching defeat from the jaws of victory involves life insurance and policy loans. Clients borrow from cash value and then surrender the policy, forgetting that they had taken a loan—with disastrous income tax results; see Howard Zaritsky, "Mallory v. Commissioner: Income Recognized on Termination of Insurance Policy with Outstanding Loans," *Steve Leimberg's Estate Planning E-mail Newsletter*, June 13, 2016.

12. For a brief discussion on stock-for-stock mergers, see Chris Gallant, "What Is a Stock-for-Stock Merger and How Does this Corporate Action Affect Existing Shareholders?" *Investopedia*. A current issue that deserves attention is the concept of portability. Portability was legislated to allow spouses to leave assets and corresponding Life Exemption to their spouses at death, thus eliminating the need for multiple trusts when the first spouse dies. However, as simple as this concept is in theory, it is fertile ground for mistakes; see Alan Gassman, Ed Morrow, Seaver Brown, and Brandon Ketron, "Ten Common Portability Mistakes and What You Need to Know to Avoid Them," *Steve Leimberg's Estate Planning Newsletter*, February 1, 2016, or Lester Law and George Karibjnian, "Top 10 Things You Should Know About the Final Portability Regulations," *Steve Leimberg's Estate Planning E-mail Newsletter*, July 9, 2015.

13. For information about Family Limited Partnerships and its younger sibling, Family Limited Liability Companies, see Pamela Savage Forbat, "Family Limited Partnerships," *Wealth Management.com*, March 1, 2000, and Andriy Blokhin, "What Is a Family Limited Liability Company (LLC)?" *Investopedia*. June 29, 2015. For the IRS view of these planning vehicles, see Paul Sullivan, "Navigating Tougher IRS Rules for Family Partnerships," *New York Times*, August 7, 2015.

14. For information about Qualified Personal Residence Trusts (QPRTs), see "Qualified Personal Residence Trust," BB&T website.

15. For LGBT individuals, see John McManus, "Top 10 Tax and Estate Planning Considerations for Same-Sex Couples," *Trusts & Estates*, June 24, 2016. For the end of File and Suspend, see Avram Sacks, "The April 29th Deadline for 'File & Suspend' Social Security Benefit Claiming Strategy," *Steve Leimberg's Employee Benefits and Retirement Planning Newsletter*, April 14, 2016, or Sharon Appelman, "The Art and Science of Claiming Social Security Benefits," *Advisor Perspectives*, March 9, 2016.

Chapter 4

The Playing Field

———————◆———————

Prologue

Unlike other chapters, in which I use a single example to lay the groundwork for what follows, this chapter requires several examples. Changes to the playing field can take many forms, and for this reason, the subject deserves broader explanation.

One of my favorite examples is a complicated one. In the game of Wealth Transfer and Distribution, one of the most challenging objectives is to be categorized as a real estate professional for income tax purposes. Although many people own investment real estate, few try to characterize themselves as real estate professionals because convincing the IRS of their qualifications is so difficult.[1] If someone doesn't meet the real estate professional standard, losses in excess of real estate income must be carried over to succeeding years as opposed to being used against other, non–real-estate sources of income (W-2, interest, dividends, capital gains, etc.). For example, let's say my properties generate $100 in revenues, but $125 in expenses and depreciation. If I lack the real estate professional designation, the $25 loss must be carried over to future years as opposed to being used to lower other income today. Sometimes this loss carryforward can't be used until the property is sold, which could take years![2]

My friend Mick was able to secure real-estate professional status. This was important to him not only because he was a real estate investor and operator, but also because he invested in real estate specifically for conservation purposes. He wanted to preserve farmland rather than allowing it to be developed into homes and shops. However, keeping farmland as farmland isn't as easy as it may seem; tax law requires that a genuine effort be made to generate revenues. In this case, Mick decided to lease his land to cattle owners for grazing while he started to build his own herds. Since this approach to building a business that encompassed a conservation objective required several years before revenues began to increase, being able to use real estate losses against non–real-estate income saved him tax dollars and thus funded his conservation efforts.

———— ♦ ————

One important trend in current transfer and distribution planning focuses on multigenerational planning: Parents leave assets to their children in trust with the provision that balances remaining at their children's deaths be transferred to grandchildren. This is at odds with the more traditional approach of leaving assets directly to the next generation. There are many reasons for multigenerational planning, but two of the more important are asset protection and tax deferral.[3]

Frank and Sally set up their estate plan so that when they pass, their assets will be available to their children but not owned by them. In effect, their children will have the benefit of access to funds but will not directly own the assets. The goal of this plan was to enable the children and grandchildren to enjoy Frank and Sally's assets without either of the later generations having to pay transfer taxes on them.

When considering this approach, Frank and Sally sought to build in asset protection and tax deferral. The asset protection comes from the fact that while their children can enjoy income from the assets and can access principal for purposes of health, support, maintenance, and education, no complete transfer occurs. Simply stated, they do not enjoy unfettered control over the assets; for example, they can't decide to give these assets away. Because Frank and Sally also stipulated that whatever was left when the children died would go to *their* children (Frank and Sally's grandchildren), they were able to use a special exemption, the Generation-Skipping Transfer Tax Exemption, thus allowing them to avoid transfer taxes at the children's passing. Through this approach, Frank and Sally made it possible for their children and grandchildren to access assets without exposing themselves to potential liability claims—due to the fact that neither the children nor the grandchildren would ever have complete control over those assets—and at the same time, they found a way to avoid transfer taxes for the next seventy to one hundred years![4]

———————— ♦ ————————

Finally, let's consider the case of Ed, age seventy-one, who wants to make a series of gifts to his college. Ed graduated fifty years ago and wants to provide an annual benefit to his college, and additional substantive funds when he dies. He doesn't want his gift to affect his income more than necessary, and he also wants to be sure that his gifts are tax-efficient and guaranteed. When he and I discussed his goals, we decided the best source of funds for these gifts was his IRA account.[5]

In 2015 Congress passed a permanent law allowing individuals older than 70½ to make charitable gifts up to $100,000 annually directly from an IRA account. This approach is preferable to other ways of gifting because there is no effect on Ed's income tax return. If he used assets other than his IRA account, Ed might need to sell these assets or to supplement them with cash and then try to balance this out on his income tax return. Since there are rules governing how assets are sold and how gifts are made, Ed could inadvertently make his gift inefficiently, resulting in unnecessary taxes. But by simply transferring funds from his IRA with no income tax or gift recognition, Ed can make a tax-neutral transaction that delivers the optimal tax result.

To achieve his long-term goal of a final gift to his school, Ed named the university as the primary beneficiary of his IRA account. This action yielded two benefits: First, it eliminated any income tax on remaining IRA funds prior to distribution—taxes that would have been imposed if Ed had left these funds to an individual. Second, it guaranteed that whatever was left in his account would go where he wished, but only after he himself had had the opportunity to enjoy it.

———————— ◆ ————————

In each of these cases, with some effort, players altered the playing field. By finding a way for Mick to be treated as a real estate professional, we improved his ability to take losses. By making use of a recent change in the law, Ed was able to achieve his charitable objectives. Finally, Frank and Sally were able to protect their assets from outside liability claims and avoid taxes for multiple generations, which gave the family the sense of control and protection they wanted.

Changing the field from what we presume it to be to what we *want* it to be should be a goal for anyone with assets to transfer and distribute. Needless to say, it isn't possible to succeed in every case, but surprising results can be accomplished with some effort and creativity.[6]

Stretching and Expanding the Playing Field

Most games have a clearly defined field of play. By contrast, the game of Wealth Transfer and Distribution has a flexible playing field, which allows the astute player to define the limits. This is a critical point that I believe is often ill understood. If the rules are narrowly applied, any game can be predefined—and a narrow definition of the playing field can be used against the player. On the other hand, when the field can be manipulated in favor of the players, so can the results.

Happily, in the game of Wealth Transfer and Distribution, it is possible to change the shape of the field. Obviously, there are limits to the degree of change that is possible, but in many cases, our field is not predefined or fixed. At the same time, the degree to which the field can be changed depends on what game we are playing. Once the player defines her goals and objectives, she can begin to shape the field.[7]

A few examples may prove helpful. As I mentioned earlier, the current annual gift exclusion is $14,000 per donor per year, although this amount may be given to as many recipients as the donor deems worthy. The rules and regulations define the value of the gift, but not what forms the gift may take. Thus, it is possible to make this gift in cash or in noncash assets. And as soon as the concept of noncash assets is introduced, it becomes possible to change the field of play. Noncash assets allow players both flexibility and opportunity.[8]

Let's say that the player wants to make of gift of stock worth $14,000 that is likely to appreciate in the future. In this case, the long-term value of the gift is prospectively greater than the value of $14,000 in cash, although the initial values are equal. However, by making a gift in kind—that is, noncash—the player not only transfers her prospects for subsequent appreciation; she also transfers her tax basis. By making the gift in noncash assets, she passes along not only the potential for appreciation, but also any embedded tax cost.

Assuming that the recipient's tax rate is significantly lower than the player's rate, this approach provides another way for the player to create a transfer benefit. By giving an asset with appreciation prospects, the player avoided the higher tax cost that would have been imposed if she had sold the asset and delivered the gift in cash. While there is still a tax associated with this gift (due on the spread between the value and the donor's basis), the recipient will net more in case of a sale—even an immediate sale—due to his lower tax bracket.

Taking this example a step further, let's say the player sought to make a gift of interest in illiquid and undivided real estate and wanted to limit the recipient's ability to monetize the asset. Even this kind of gift is possible. Here the recipient has received something of value, but it can't easily be sold. Sometimes this type of gift carries the greatest long-term value due to its barriers to disposition. Sales limitations can force the recipient to hold onto an asset and subsequently allow it to reach its highest value. In these examples, we stretched and expanded the playing field to meet our objective.

While we can expand the playing field, we aren't just limited to changing the character of what we do. Assume that we have two goals for our daughter, Jane: make a gift of $14,000 and also pay her graduate-school tuition. At first glance, it may seem that we are bounded by the rules and regulations, and thereby restricted to one activity. In fact, we can make both gifts by making the cash gift to Jane and paying the tuition payment directly to the school. This is due to an exception in the regulations. What appeared at first glance to be impossible can be achieved by understanding the rules and applying them to our playing field. In this case, the ability to assist Jane required us to understand two things: the limits of gifting in general, and the exceptions to those same gifting rules.[9]

Complex Changes

Interestingly, sometimes the more complex our goals, the more malleable the field of play. While this may seem counterintuitive, it shouldn't be. Consider building a baseball stadium: While there are certain defined requirements (four bases ninety feet apart; a pitching mound sixty feet, six inches from home plate; and straight foul lines down both the first and third base lines), the rest of the park is largely subject to the owner's whims. There are no predefined requirements for the outfield walls, as evidenced by the Green Monster in Boston and the ivy-covered walls at Wrigley Field. Similarly, there can be huge or small foul-ball areas, and there can be cavernous outfields or short porches.[1*] The point is that after the basic requirements are met, the owner has considerable leeway in the design of the rest of the field.

We have similar circumstances in the game of Wealth Transfer and Distribution. While there are rules and regulations that must be followed, they generally stipulate minimums and maximums. Apart from those stipulations, the player is given room to be creative. In baseball, we can't have outfield walls that move; they must be in the same place for both teams so that neither team has an advantage. The same is not the case in Wealth Transfer and Distribution; we are not obliged to be consistent.

---

1   *A baseball term: When one of the outfield walls is unusually close to home plate, a stadium is said to have a "short porch."

Since we are oftentimes playing against the rule book, as opposed to another team, we can change the field to meet our needs on a case-by-case basis. In other words, we can move the fences in one case and leave them as they are in another. This is where the arguments of form over substance and substance over form come into play. By narrowly defining our approach using form over substance, we can limit the field of play because we place the focus on the letter of the law. In another case, we can choose to expand the field as much as needed by arguing substance over form, because we are trying to broaden the application of the law.

What begins as a simple set of objectives often becomes more complicated and demanding upon closer examination. Many times I have heard a client say, "All I want to do is …" Unfortunately, what seems to the client like a simple goal is in fact a mind-bender that requires the field to be reshaped, sometimes more than once in the course of the process, to accommodate her wishes. When this happens, it is crucial for the player and the team to take the time to understand clearly what they are doing to the field of play, lest by making one change they set off a series of unforeseen and undesired additional changes.

For example, suppose we have a player—let's call him Don—who wants to pass ownership of the family business to his son Barry, who is active in the business.[10] On its face, this is a simple desire. However, the business is the primary family asset and Don wants to treat all three children equally. Thus, some accommodation needs to be made for the other children. Unfortunately, these two children hate each other, don't trust each other, and can't work together on even the simplest of matters. Moreover, Grandma's trust has already divided her 30 percent share of the company between them, giving each of them 15 percent. Due to this complex state of affairs, passing the entire business to the actively involved son requires a number of steps.

First, Don ideally needs to convince the nonparticipating children to transfer their interests to their brother Barry, which in turn requires Barry to have the means to buy their interests, and the other children, to be willing to sell. Second, Don needs to have assets of adequate value that he can gift to his other children in order to meet his objective of equal treatment.

Complicating matters even further, one of the nonparticipating children, Lily, wants to sell her interest in the business *today*, despite the fact that her brother doesn't presently have the funds on hand to buy her out. This impatient daughter is threatening to gift her stock to her own daughter, Penelope—a minor who was born out of wedlock and is controlled by her birth father— unless her demand is met. Finally, Don happens to live in a house owned by the corporation and won't leave this house until he dies.

Needless to say, in a case like this, "all I want to do" is not as simple as it sounds. The actual process necessarily must reshape the field in a way that takes all the attendant interests and problems into account—a challenge even for the best team of specialists. In a case like this, we may be looking at a game that lasts several years before all objectives are met.[11]

How does the owner react when told that his simple wish is going to require a herculean effort? Naturally, he expresses disappointment and frustration. After all, the reason he has this manager, these coaches, and all these specialists is to win the game he's playing. Unfortunately, since we do not have the right field of play, we need to see how we can recast the field to accommodate the owner's wishes, and this takes time. The good news is that it is not necessary to rebuild the entire park to achieve the desired results. A few changes to the field of play might deliver some immediate results and set the stage for the desired end results.

Modifying the field of play requires the owner to realize that some changes to his goals may need to be considered. For example, we can ask Don if equal distribution is really necessary; there is, after all, a difference between equal and approximate. Since Barry is working in the business, some of the company's growth might be attributable to his efforts. If this is the case, perhaps distribution among the children can be modified to account for his contributions. Or perhaps Don can lend Barry funds to buy out Lily's ownership interest today and thereby end the threat of Penelope's father being involved in the company's affairs.

Once these kinds of considerations have been explored, progress can be made. However, it is important to ask a simple question: After we have achieved our immediate objectives, what else can we see coming down the road? What if, as is often the case, this set of goals is only part of the family's overall objectives? Do we intend the changes we're making to the field of play to be temporary? Or are we going to have to undo what we've done in order to move on to other family objectives?

Since our game is played on paper, we don't have the same landscaping concerns as the owners of a ballpark. Nevertheless, our game must operate in a coherent fashion. We need to be sure that our return to the normal field of play is seamless, and we need to know what that field will look like after the changes have been made. Every effort must be made to ensure that changes made to the field of play today don't interfere with other efforts tomorrow.

For example, assume that Don arranges a loan from the corporation to help Barry buy out his sisters—but the business uses the house in which Don resides for collateral. Further assume that the business experiences a downturn in profits and the bank calls its loan, requiring the sale of the house that Don calls home. Although we will have accomplished a great deal by taking ownership of the business out of the hands of the nonparticipating children and eliminating the threat of a nonfamily shareholder, we will have failed to meet Don's only personal objective: remaining in his home until his death. Clearly, it is essential to anticipate all the potential ramifications of change to the playing field.

———— ♦ ————

Another set of challenges can occur when an owner, after years of playing a simple game on a cookie-cutter playing field, decides to complicate his plans. Let's say that someone is considering divorce and remarriage, and he will need not only to provide for his first wife for the remainder of her life, but also to meet the requirements of his second wife and her children for the rest of his own life.[12]

In this case there are a number of issues requiring attention, because if our client does this, he effectively tears down the old ballpark and puts up a new one loaded with bells and whistles. Simple elegance gives way to ornate complication, and a low-cost field requiring only basic maintenance turns into an expensive stadium requiring constant oversight and review. When such a dramatic change occurs, it is necessary to move forward carefully.

The most important question to ask and answer before changing the field of play is *why*. Why do you want to make this change, what do you expect to accomplish, and are you really ready to pay the price? In this case it is essential that the owner and manager clearly understand their capacity to accommodate change. Drastic change can result in the need for a new set of coaches and a new group of specialists, all of whom come at a cost.[13]

Such change is acceptable so long as the player, the manager, and the coaches understand the limits of their abilities. Unfortunately, in many cases the team lacks this understanding, which becomes a problem for the owner. When the owner switches gears and moves to a new field of play, he must be sure that his support team can still meet his needs. In my experience, such changes are seldom accompanied by the necessary careful review and consideration; in most cases the existing manager and coaches continue doing everything, assuming—incorrectly—that they can adapt to meet the new challenges.

For the owner this is one of the most critical points in the game. When she changes the field of play, especially by taking on additional complexity and more demanding tasks, she must know that her on-field manager and coaches can make the change along with her. How can she be sure of this? By getting a second opinion and challenging her assumptions. That second opinion can come from a friendly competitor; it can come from a retired player who shared similar interests and objectives; it can even come from outside consultants. But it must come from somewhere.

Changing the field of play, especially by introducing greater complexity, requires the player to question the ability of the manager and coaching staff to fulfill their new responsibilities. Not all teams are built the same way. In baseball, for example, some teams are built for speed, and others, for power, and when a speed team moves to a park built for a power team, they must adjust their strategy. If your team is not suitable—that is, if they are a speed team that cannot adapt to a power park—then they will have to be replaced. Of course, it may turn out that the existing staff is suitable . . . but is suitability sufficient? It's my opinion that the manager and coaching staff must be more than "suitable" for the new field of play—they must be *ideally* suited to it. If they aren't, the owner is apt to get mediocre results.

Failure on the part of the owner to challenge managers and coaching staff when changing the field of play is one of the more common causes of disappointment. There is a distinct difference between playing catch and playing baseball. If the owner's desire is merely to toss assets around by making annual cash gifts of $14,000 per recipient (a simple game of catch), then the manager and coaches need not be of the highest quality. On the other hand, if the owner wants to play for keeps by making complicated gifts like the business transfer above, then the on-field manager and coaching staff must be of the highest quality, as this kind of game requires the right playing field and the right players. It also requires discipline and risk management. The costliest error an owner can make is to change the playing field but to retain the current staff. When goals and objectives change, and when these changes affect the field of play, the required level of knowledge and sophistication usually increases.[14]

The field of play is, in my opinion, one of the most overlooked considerations in the game of Wealth Transfer and Distribution. Using the field of play to its best advantage increases the owner's ability to succeed and grow. On the other hand, failing to understand that altering the field of play requires more than landscaping modifications can be fatal. Defining the playing field is critical, and it is of the utmost importance to ensure that your field is shaped to your advantage.[15]

Notes

1. Peter J. Reilly, "Real Estate Professional Status—Becoming More Important—Very Hard to Prove," *Forbes*, January 27, 2013. Also see John H. Skarbnik, "Real Estate Professionals: Avoiding the Passive Activity Loss Rules," *The Tax Adviser*, June 30, 2014. To see what process the IRS imposes on a taxpayer, see "Audit Technique Guides—Passive Activity Losses," IRS Publication, January 7, 2016.
2. For an introduction to passive activity losses, see Barbara Cruz, "Using Suspended Passive Activity Losses," *TidyTax*, July 3, 2013. To see the full force of the IRS on passive activity loses, see IRS Publication 925, *Passive Activity and At-Risk Rules*.
3. Another major reason for multigenerational planning is the use of discounts to reduce the value of gifts. However, proposed regulations to Section 2704 of the Internal Revenue Code (IRC) are threatening the use of discounts in the future. As such, while discounts are highly

attractive in multigenerational planning, there is concern that their advantages may become a thing of the past. See Mitchell Gans and Jonathan G. Blattmachr, "Recently Proposed Section 2704 Regulations," *Steve Leimberg's Estate Planning Newsletter*, August 5, 2016, and Steve Oshins and Bob Keebler, "Creative Planning Strategies Once 2704 Regs Become Final," *Steve Leimberg's Estate Planning Newsletter*, August 8, 2016. For a summary article, see Jonathan G. Blattmachr and Mitchell M. Gans, "Treasury Issues Broad Proposed 2704 Regulations," *Wealthmanagement.com*, August 3, 2016, or Allyson Versprille, "IRS Expected to Face Pushback Against New Estate Tax Rules," *Wealthmanagement.com*, August 9, 2016.

4. Lest anyone think that intra-family gifting is chump change, see "Tax-Free Gifts Quadrupled after IRS Limit Lifted," *Bloomberg News*, January 29, 2014. In 2012 Americans reported **$122 billion** in nontaxable gifts. This amount doesn't take into account non-reportable gifts—that is, those gifts equal to or less than the Annual Exclusion, currently at $14,000 per recipient. At the same time, there is appropriate concern over leaving vast sums (or even small sums) of money to children whose character is yet unformed. For ways to plan around this, see Robert Pagliarini, "5 Tips for Leaving Your Children Money," *Forbes*, May 12, 2014. The same concerns apply to senior citizens who are potentially at risk for elder abuse; see "New Rules for Protection of Seniors Are Being Considered," *Trust Advisor*, November 4, 2015. For a factual discussion of one parent's decision making, see Ross Toback and Julia Marsh, "Daughters Inherit $20M, but There's a Catch," *New York Post*, July 27, 2015. In addition, it is also possible to create perpetual trusts; for a brief overview of a case which endorsed perpetual trusts, see Steve Oshins, "Bullion Monarch Mining, Inc. v. Barrick Goldstrike Mines: Unconstitutional Perpetual Trusts—Not So Fast Says the Nevada Supreme Court!" *Steve Leimberg's Estate Planning Newsletter*, April 6, 2015, and Steve Oshins, "The Rebuttal to Unconstitutional Perpetual Trusts," *Steve Leimberg's Estate Planning Newsletter*, December 22, 2014. Finally, no discussion would be complete without at least a general reference to Family Limited Liability Companies and Family Limited Partnerships; again, there is a surplus of information on these topics, but they are critical components in any player's ability to change the field in family planning!

5. Conrad Teitell, "'Legacy IRA' Bill Would Authorize Charitable Life-Income IRA Rollovers," *Steve Leimberg's Charitable Planning Newsletter*, May 18, 2016, and Richard Fox, "IRA Charitable Rollover Provision Made Permanent and Retroactive to January 1, 2015," *Steve Leimberg's Charitable Planning Newsletter*, December 21, 2015.

6. Martin M. Shenkman, "Not Your Granddad's Trust," *Financial Planning*, January 2016, pages 32–33. Even roles within legal documents have expanded over time, as have remedies for altering trusts more favorably.

7. Change can be more than transactional; it can be expanded to include family traditions. Tanya Tucker, "Help Your Clients Save Money by Remaking Traditions," *Trust Advisor*, January 27, 2016.

8. For a highly readable explanation of gifts, see "Frequently Asked Questions on Gift Taxes," IRS Publication.

9. Jenna Ichikawa, "Gift Tax Exclusion for Payment of Qualifying Medical and Tuition Expenses," Stokes Lawrence Law Firm website.

10. Russell Alan Prince and Brett Van Bortel, "Helping Middle-Market Family Businesses," *Financial Advisor*, October 1, 2015. Issues concerning family businesses are critical to the game of Wealth Transfer and Distribution because about two-thirds of all businesses *are* family businesses.

11. For a handy list of to-dos that everyone should consider, see David A. Handler and Kristen A. Curatolo, "Twenty Tips for Planning at the Eleventh Hour," *Wealthmanagement. com*, June 13, 2016, or "8 Red Flags That Your Clients' Estate Plans Are Out of Whack," *Wealthmanagement.com*, August 5, 2016. In most cases there are actions that can be taken

that can help transfer/distribution plans. At the same time, it must be remembered that tax avoidance is permissible within the law; see Brooke Harrington, "Inside the Secretive World of Tax-Avoidance Experts," *The Atlantic*, October 26, 2015. For a practical example of how a good situation could have been made better, see Bruce Steiner, "Lessons from Frank Gifford's Will," *Steve Leimberg's Estate Planning Newsletter*, November 5, 2015.

12. Not only does divorce makes life difficult and complicated, so does the changing definition of marriage. The increasing prevalence of same-sex marriages has had a significant impact on how marriage is interpreted both federally and by states; see Carlyn S. McCaffrey and John C. McCaffrey, "*Obergefell* and the Authority of the IRS to Challenge Valid Marriages and Divorces," *Steve Leimberg's Estate Planning E-mail Newsletter*, September 15, 2015. For married couples, a major obstacle to planning is portability, a topic that merits a separate book. Portability provides the surviving spouse the opportunity to absorb the deceased spouse's Lifetime Exemption for use when the surviving spouse dies. Since there are many resources available on this topic, it may make sense to a see how a set of wait-and-see approaches can provide additional flexibility to the survivor; see James M. Kane, "Opt-In or Opt-Out Planning for Under $10 Million Married Couples," *Steve Leimberg's Estate Planning E-mail Newsletter*, January 23, 2014.

13. Even states compete for advantages when it comes to the game of Wealth Transfer and Distribution; for an overview, see Patricia Cohen, "States Vie to Shield Wealth of the 1 Percent," *New York Times*, August 8, 2016. For more specific information, see Neil Schoenblum and Steven J. Oshins, "The Nevada Advantage: Why Nevada Has Become the Leading Jurisdiction for Trusts," *Trust Advisor*, May 25, 2016; Steve Oshins, "3rd Annual Trust Decanting States Rankings Chart," *Steve Leimberg's Estate Planning Newsletter*, January 7, 2016; Steve Oshins, "First Inter-Active Dynasty Trust State Rankings Chart," *Steve Leimberg's Estate Planning Newsletter*, October 8, 2015; and Steve Oshins, "6th annual Domestic Asset Protection State Rankings," *Steve Leimberg's Asset Protection Planning E-mail Newsletter*, May 4, 2015. Some states are late to the game; see Jonathan E. Gopman et al., "West Virginia Passes Asset Protection Trust Legislation Effective June 8, 2016," *Steve Leimberg's Asset Protection Planning E-mail Newsletter*, June 8, 2016. Also see Ben Lee, "New Bill to Ease Access to Client Accounts After Death," *Trust Advisor*, January 25, 2016. Asset classes are also subject to change; see Lacey Kessler, "Alternative Investments Aren't Just for the Rich," *Trust Advisor*, May 18, 2016; Reel Ken, "Master Limited Partnerships: Sifting Through the Wreckage," *Seeking Alpha*, April 17, 2016. To understand better the ebbs and flows of investment markets as a source for investing alternatives, see Henry Blodgett, "Market History Is Calling, and It's Saying Stock Performance Will Be Crappy for Another 10 Years," *Business Insider*, October 4, 2015. In addition to asset classes changing, there is a concerted focus on dividend-based investing, especially given the need for income and the desire to transfer and distribute assets downstream; for the basics of dividend investing, see M. Alden, "Dividend Growth Investing 101," *Dividend Monk*, October 6, 2010.

14. For an example of how bad things can get when the train leaves the tracks, see Jonathan E. Gopman et al., "*In re Ferrante:* Not Modifying Trust to Comply with Tax Law Creates Bankruptcy Nightmare," *Steve Leimberg's Asset Protection Planning E-mail Newsletter*, November 10, 2015.

15. Lacey Kessler, "Pet Trusts—They're Not Just for Crazy Billionaire Tax Evaders," *Trust Advisor*, June 24, 2016 and Steven Maimes, "Pet Trust States Grow as Owners Continue to Leave Money to Care for their Dogs and Cats," *Trust Advisor*, May 20, 2016. Expanding the playing field can result in brand-new considerations which, given changing attitudes in America toward pets, can lead to entirely new planning ideas. At the other end of transfer and distribution is the issue of how to deal with art; see Darren M. Wallace and Alexis Getter, "Using Family Entities for Planning with Artwork," *Trusts & Estates*, June 2016,

pages 27–31. For other potential changes to the planning landscape, see Lee Slavutin, "A Post-*Morrissette* Roadmap for Drafting Intergenerational Split-Dollar Agreements," *Steve Leimberg's Estate Planning Newsletter*, May 12, 2016; Mary Vandenack and Nicholas Meier, "Assisting Clients with Gun Trusts," *Steve Leimberg's Estate Planning Newsletter*, May 3, 2016.

Chapter 5

Building Your Team

Prologue

n the game of Wealth Transfer and Distribution, putting together the right team is critical. Team building starts with family members and continues through to finding the right long-term and short-term players to complete the team's roster. These long-term and short-term players include various types of attorneys, accountants, bankers, insurance brokers, and investment advisors, as well as lesser-used players like trust officers, fiduciaries, realtors, and valuation experts. Great teams build strong rosters and use their resources to generate the best results.[1]

One family that clearly understands the benefits of team building is headed by a dear friend of mine, Michael. I started working with Michael and his parents more than thirty years ago. When we started working together, the family had modest ambitions: Michael wanted to make sure that his parents were cared for and that the small family trucking business he operated with his father, Harry, would last.

Families with businesses tend to have some children who work in the business and others who, for whatever reasons, choose not to work in the business. This family was no different—Michael worked in the business, but his two sisters did not—and one of the family's primary goals was to ensure that all of the children, whether they were in the business or not, were treated as fairly as possible. To achieve this goal, the family hired an attorney who was especially skilled at putting together family distribution plans.

Once this objective was identified, the next step was to make sure the assets Harry and his wife owned could be passed intact to his Michael and his sisters. Since there were potential tax issues, Michael, Harry, the attorney, and I found a tax accountant who knew how to identify and plan against tax liabilities. As a result of the tax analysis performed by this accountant, the family concluded that it would be beneficial for Harry and his wife to make provisions for transfer taxes (a more polite term for death costs) upon their passing.

When Harry and his wife died fifteen years later, we finalized the first phase of the family's plans. We used predesignated funds from insurance policies to handle the taxes, and we set up a financial support system for Michael's sisters and took steps to ensure that the business passed to Michael. While this met the first generation's goals, our work had just begun.

Michael wanted to expand his business and open additional locations. To do this, we needed to grow his team. Michael and his wife, Mary, concluded that they too wanted to pass their business interests to their children when the time came. Unlike Harry, however, they wanted to make some of these transitions while they were alive. What was particularly interesting about their decision was that they identified this goal from the outset. In other words, they wanted to make sure that as their business fortunes grew, they had the means in place to transfer ownership to the next generation. This goal required an attorney with a broader skill set, so Michael and Mary sought out a new team member. At the same time, they concluded that they needed a more sophisticated banking relationship than they presently had because they were going to need access to more complicated and aggressive financing. As a result, a new player was added to the team.

Michael and Mary gave their children every opportunity to decide whether or not they wanted to be in the family business. As it turned out, their daughters wanted to be in the business immediately. Their sons, on the other hand, were less certain. Michael and Mary never penalized their sons for delaying their decisions, however; they left the door open for their sons and worked with me, the attorney, and the accountant to preserve the sons' rights and opportunities.

After several years of other employment and fatherhood, both sons decided that they wanted to join the team on a full-time basis. One of the more compelling reasons for them to rejoin the team was that they could so without penalty. The family, as a group, had decided that providing options for the sons without penalty was important. Once all the family players were on board, Michael and Mary decided to begin transferring business responsibility and ownership to their children.

By this time, the family business had grown significantly. Valuing family businesses at any time is difficult, and valuing family businesses for lifetime gifting purposes is especially challenging. To make sure that we handled this properly, we needed to add specialists to the advisory team—so we found two valuation experts. One of these experts valued the business as a going concern, while the other calculated the effect of giving slices of the business to the children. Once the valuations were complete, Michael and Mary were able to meet their next objective: transferring significant ownership interests in the businesses to their children and enjoying the benefits of these efforts by securing a lifelong cash stream for themselves.

Looking back at my relationship with this family, I have worked with three separate generations, a number of professional advisors, financial and business specialists, and various sets of changing—but clear—family goals and objectives. The end result of good team building is that families are able to achieve their objectives without discord or hard feelings. In this case, our efforts served the founders (Harry and his wife), the second generation (Michael and his sisters), and the third generation (Michael and Mary's children). What started as a small family business with a modest future is now a multistate business with national ambitions run by a generation of children who are ready for the next thirty years.[2]

Team building has a critical purpose: to bring together the people necessary to get what we have to whom we want, when we want, how we want. Done properly, team building allows the players to reach both their goals and their personal potential.[3]

The Composition of Your Team

In the game of Wealth Transfer and Distribution, the player has two choices: Play the game unassisted or play the game supported by others. In my opinion, the more successful approach is the team approach, but let's not dismiss the solitary approach without explanation. It is possible to play the game alone. Based on my experience, the one-person approach succeeds most often under two circumstances: an uncomplicated distribution plan or a genius player. If the circumstances are simple, the one-man band works.[4]

Let's assume that you are well versed in the disciplines of tax, law, accounting, philanthropy, banking, risk management, investments, and financial modeling. With these talents, a single person could manage both simple distributions and complex transfers.[5] I have never met anyone who fulfilled these criteria, but it would be wrong to assume that someone like this doesn't exist. For most players, however, I believe that building the necessary support to guide the team is one of the keys to winning the game.

Given the range of talents necessary to accomplish every step of a complicated wealth transfer without help, it makes sense to locate professionals who bring these skills to the table. However, as important as these talents are to ultimate success, they are only complements to a highly effective team.[6]

The most important members of the team are you and your significant other—your primary teammate.[7] The player is the most important participant of all, of course, because he or she wears myriad hats: founder, current player, leader, immediate beneficiary, and owner. Whether the primary teammate is a spouse, the extended family, a specific child, a sibling, a parent, a friend, or even a charity, that person or entity works in concert with the player to set the tone for the game, and all other supports are secondary. Oftentimes, the player and the primary teammate (whose identity can change depending on the objectives of the immediate distribution or transfer) dictate the roles and relative importance of everyone else.[8]

In the most successful wealth transfers and distributions, the level of communication and understanding between these two players often determines success or failure. The player and the primary teammate share a relationship that allows them to talk and hear at the highest level. They must to be honest to a fault and yet continue to enjoy each other's trust and friendship. The player and his or her primary set the goals that dictate how the team will be built around them.[9]

This is no different from what we see in sports. The owner of a football team employs a general manager whose job is to bring to the field the collection of coaches and players that management believes will give them the best chance of winning. When this is done properly, and when there is clarity about goals, the ability of the owner and general manager to agree upon and work toward those goals can signal the difference between failure and success. It is no different in the game we play.

The Discrete Roles of the Team Members

While the owner/general manager model and the husband/wife model may seem different, I would suggest that there are similarities. In most marriages, one person generally plays the role of owner while the other handles the tasks of general manager. For my clients who are age sixty or older, the husband usually takes the owner role while the wife assumes the general manager role—although there are instances, most often among younger clients, in which the owner is the wife and the general manager is the husband.

With this arrangement settled, it is clear to me that the best results are secured when the shared roles of owner and general manager are harmonious. When these two players see the game the same way, identifying goals becomes easier, and the process of achieving desired results, more efficient.[10]

So how hard is it to achieve this concord? Sometimes it happens with great ease. I have seen moms and dads come to agreement on their wishes on very complicated matters within minutes. On the other hand, I have seen couples take years to agree on what seem to be simple decisions; a classic example is the selection of guardians for minor children, which has held up many an estate plan! Even when the owner/general manager team functions well, however, they need other teammates.

The first group of teammates includes the on-field manager, coaches, and specialists. These are the team members who ensure that the owner/general manager's wishes are translated to the field of play. The second group comprises the participants: family members, business associates, charities, and even outsiders. This chapter focuses on the first group because these are the folks who will make active contributions to the process, whereas the second group tends to be made up of passive individuals who clearly have roles, but whose roles are limited in nature and typically incidental to the first group's goals and objectives.

Following the owner and general manager, the person most essential to success is the on-field manager—although in some cases, this person may be more analogous to a quarterback. Irrespective of which term we use, this person usually has several key attributes. First, he can talk with and listen to the owner at the highest level. Second, he has the capacity to be candid and direct, whether you like what he says or not. Finally, this is a person you trust and rely on. In other words, the on-field manager operates as one of your closest advisors, your *consigliere*. Usually this is not a family member, as it is important to avoid emotional considerations that might cloud business relationships. The on-field manager becomes your eyes and ears when it comes to making wealth transfer and distribution decisions. As such, the on-field manager must enjoy the owner's and general manager's highest confidence. This is probably the most important nonfamily role on the team.[11]

In addition, the on-field manager needs the capacity to deal with the other team members—coaches, specialists, other players—and every kind of opposition. It is not enough for the on-field manager merely to understand the owner's goals and objectives; he or she must have the ability to translate these goals and objectives into terms meaningful to everyone else. In my experience, the owners who choose the right on-field manager shorten the time necessary to succeed and reduce the cost of success.[12]

Successful, long-term on-field managers are hard to find. With more than half a million financial advisors in America, plus countless attorneys and accountants, the talent pool is huge. Many candidates are educated, qualified, licensed, certified, experienced, recommended, and endorsed. They have achieved incredible results—they have led their companies in sales, received accolades from fellow professionals, been recognized by national publications as leaders in their fields, and received almost every honor short of a Nobel Prize. But background, experience, and recognition alone don't qualify somebody to be an on-field manager. In my opinion, hiring an on-field manager based on these qualifications alone is a big mistake.[13]

The Importance of Trust and Connection

Who has the potential to be a great on-field manager? It can be any of a number of people: the player's best friend, business partner, attorney, accountant, or financial advisor. In some cases, owners with strong religious convictions use their spiritual advisors. Irrespective of who is chosen, the two qualities most necessary for success, in my opinion, are trust and emotional resonance. It may surprise the reader that experience or knowledge aren't at the top of the list, but to me, trust is critical to the on-field manager's relationship with the owner and general manager. Without trust, there is little likelihood of success. I have seen many owners reject great ideas from knowledgeable and successful proponents because the owner lacked trust.[14]

Equally important, especially in bad times, is emotional resonance; the owner and general manager must *like* their on-field manager as much as they trust him or her. When times get tough, when crisis looms, trust is not enough; there has to be some emotional tie that binds the on-field manager to the owner and general manager in a way that transcends trust. All parties must believe that no matter how bad things get, they will cover one another.[15] Knowledge and experience are extremely important, but they aren't enough. In this game, the emotional underpinnings are as important as the tangible qualities . . . and to me, *more* important. Skills can be acquired, but trust and emotional resonance with the owner and general manager must be earned and nurtured. This is not say that trust and affection can't be developed over time, but without owner trust and emotional commitment, any on-field manager is on shaky ground.

During the Great Recession of 2008–2009, while other firms rushed to explain the financial disruptions to their clients, my firm was lucky. We had spent years cultivating our clients' trust and friendship, and we augmented this deeper layer of client involvement with knowledge and experience. We proactively advised clients early of what might happen, told them when what we'd suspected *could* happen *had* happened, and then laid out how we, as their on-field managers, were going to do our level best to ensure that their objectives were met. While our clients were deeply concerned, they knew we had their backs. Obviously, there was no way for us to completely mitigate the effects of the recession, but our experience and our bond of trust reassured our clients that we could still field a winning team. While other teams were firing their on-field managers, we retained our positions. Not only that, we actually strengthened our relationships with existing clients and attracted new ones who were intrigued by our way of playing the game. In many cases, the owner's concern was limited to a single question: "Am I all right?" Since we could affirmatively answer that question, the impact of the recession was diminished and we were able to focus our energies on playing the game.

The Relationship between the General Manager and the On-Field Manager

So what happens once the owner and general manager select their on-field manager? Assuming the manager succeeds, the relationship grows. It begins with goals that evolve and develop over time as existing goals are accomplished and new ones set.

But something else happens as well: Everyone grows older together. I have seen this in my own experience. Clients from thirty years ago are thirty years older, as am I. One of the hallmarks of these successful relationships over time is that working together enhances and strengthens the relationship. Essentially, people start thinking similarly and anticipating one another's needs and wants.[16]

In the spirit of trust and emotional resonance, the owner, general manager, and on-field manager must plan for on-field management succession in a more detailed way than we plan for owner or general-manager succession.

Since the owner and general manager may be related parties while the on-field manager is not, it is essential that the on-field manager have a clear understanding of his or her limitations, especially limitations brought on by age or changing interests. It is necessary to groom for success at every level of the team, but nowhere is it more important than in these three roles, and of the three, it is the manager whose departure and replacement can oftentimes be the most unsettling. Since owner and general-manager succession is most often an in-house transaction, it can be accommodated more easily over time. With a change of on-field manager, on the other hand, there is usually a period of dislocation and unease while all parties learn to work comfortably together. For this reason, owners and general managers often delay this decision as long as possible. In fact, sometimes owners and general managers prefer to wait until a succeeding generation is ready to assume top-line responsibility before making a managerial change. This is done specifically to ensure a complete change of management. However, this decision-making process carries its own liability: Unless the heirs are ready to assume responsibility, the decision to change the entire management structure can be challenging, even disastrous. In the best circumstances, the grooming of future owners and general managers occurs naturally because the family is motivated to sustain its success by selecting a capable manager. In the worst of circumstances, however, avoidance of decisions and neglect of training can put a family's future at risk.[17]

For all these reasons there must be realistic expectations of how long the on-field manager can continue to be effective. Even when the on-field manager is new to the team, every effort must be made to determine what will be done if something happens to him; nothing damages a team more than unexpectedly losing a highly effective manager. In addition, even the best relationships can lose their effectiveness over time. A responsible on-field manager needs to question his or her own effectiveness and be ready to walk away from a great relationship before it devolves into a merely good relationship.

Coaches

While the on-field manager is critical to the team's success, he cannot operate alone. Most managers need coaches and specialists who can anticipate team needs before they occur. The best on-field managers surround themselves with people who are as talented as they are (or more so) in certain areas. These people are the team's coaches.[18]

Coaches are required for specific tasks in wealth transfer and distribution. In most cases, the initial coaching staff numbers about four; the staff will usually include an estate attorney, a business attorney, a certified public accountant, and a financial advisor. In some cases, a banker may fill the role of a coach. These coaches serve essentially the same purpose that an athletic coach serves for a sports team: to provide motivation and feedback so that the player is not left to figure out on his own how best to improve his game. A good athletic coach can spot the weaknesses in the player's form and offer suggestions for improvement: "Choke up on that bat a little and move your left foot back! Put your shoulder into it! That was perfect; now give me ten more laps!" Similarly, a coach employed to improve your Wealth Transfer and Distribution game will ask important questions and make appropriate suggestions: "With a new child on the way, should you consider more insurance?" "Now that you've gotten a raise, should you open an IRA account?" When I coach my clients, I often recommend things they have never heard of and probably wouldn't have heard of if not for me. That's the value of a coach.[19]

At the highest level, coaching becomes much more refined. If Tiger Woods can have a swing coach, so should I, if I can afford one. Most people play the game at half speed (or less) because they don't know how to accelerate what they're doing. And as a result, they get much less out of their normal circumstances than they should. It's similar to driving a car and never getting out of second gear: You want to go faster, but you don't know how, and by trying to go faster in second gear, you're actually hurting the car and hindering your performance.

It is not necessary or wise for the manager to do everything, but it *is* necessary for the manager to assume responsibility for outcomes. This means the manager must be able to identify talent when choosing coaches, and must be equally able to see when mismatches occur. The issue is not identifying the positions to be filled; it's filling the positions with the right people. While the best on-field managers occupy stable positions for years or decades, the same is not true of the coaches they hire. Coaches must come and go at times. Obviously, the ideal team would be one on which the owner, general manager, on-field manager, and coaches could work together forever, but in reality, this seldom happens. One requirement for the manager is to know when the team has outgrown a coach and make the necessary change.[20]

Being let go is not necessarily a criticism of the coach. For example, suppose the coach who needs to be dismissed is your banker. Many banks today have more restrictive lending guidelines than they did ten years ago, and rather than trying to get a bank to make constant exceptions to these guidelines, it might be better to move to another bank where the parameters are less restrictive. In this example, the team's needs don't reflect badly on the banker; it's a matter of the present coach being unable to provide the team with what it needs. Obviously, the manager wants to be forward-looking when finding coaches, but exogenous events sometimes occur, and needs quickly change. For the on-field manager to best meet the team's needs, coaches sometimes need to be replaced.

Specialization

It is critical to use coaches to their best purpose. In football, for example, it makes no sense for the running back's coach to assume responsibility for the defensive line. Likewise in baseball, a pitching coach's talents would be wasted at third base. In wealth transfer and distribution matters, however, it is not unusual for coaches to perform functions outside their skill sets . . . often with regrettable results. There are times in the relationship between the on-field manager and a particular coach when the manager asks the coach to perform a function that is outside his or her area of competence. What a good coach needs to do in a case like this is decline the task and tell the manager that either another coach or a specialist is better suited.

Specialists—coaches with uncommon expertise in specific fields—are extremely beneficial to wealth transfer and distribution issues. For example, while a tax accountant may be great at identifying tax issues, he may not be the right candidate for a tax court case. In this instance, it might be better to bring in a tax attorney who specializes in litigation. This is akin to bringing in a putting specialist for a golfer whose game is off. While her regular swing coach can assist in most aspects of her game, there are times when someone who specializes in tuning up putting strokes can be a big asset.[21]

This harks back to our discussion of suitability in chapter 4; depending upon the game played, the specialist used may vary. While a football coach may be a defensive genius, he may be ill-suited to build a formidable basketball defense. For each game the player plays, he or she must determine which defensive specialist is best suited to protect the turf at risk (see chapter 7 for a more in-depth discussion of defensive play). Team owners often see specialists as more versatile than they truly are, but they are not a substitute for the on-field manager, and they are certainly not replacements for the regular coaches. They are tools to be used for specific purposes, depending on the game being played. After their task is completed, they are relieved of daily duty. A great specialist is one who knows her limits and advises the owner and player when those limits have been reached. A bad specialist is one who believes that his solution is appropriate for any game. Making sure your specialists stay within their areas of expertise is one of the greatest challenges to a team owner and player.

Another benefit to bringing in specialists is that doing so can actually be cheaper and more effective than relying on your regular coaching staff to figure things out. When circumstances arise that require a specialist, my recommendation is to secure the right one as soon as possible; it's the best way to get the player's game back on track.[22]

Making Your Team Gel

Putting together the group that will actually support the team is the one of the most important initial steps. Until this is done, it makes little sense to move forward. With the right on-field manager, coaches, and specialists, Mom and Dad can be positioned to look at what they want to do.

Cohesion is an area in which team-building often falls short despite the general manager's best efforts. Collegiality is one of the most important aspects of the team-building process; the coaches must respect one another and be willing to listen to alternate points of view. In my experience, the best results are achieved by teams whose coaches understand that they complement one another, as opposed to feeling the need to protect their positions. When turf warfare breaks out, it almost always signals the need for one coach to leave in order to preserve harmony among the coaches. Even the best coach isn't worth having if conflict follows in his wake. Since the game of Wealth Transfer and Distribution is not a game of precision, it is better sometimes to accept a little less creativity in order to get things done.

As a final comment on building support for your team, I want to reinforce a point I made earlier in discussing the role of the on-field manager: Just as it is necessary for the owner to like and trust the on-field manager, it is also necessary for management to like and trust the coaches. Trust is essential; after all, the on-field manager is putting the success of the team in the hands of the coaches. The on-field manager manages the coaches, and the coaches manage the players. It is essential for management to like its coaches, to see them as necessary and welcome contributors to the team's success. I have seen trust shaken when problems arise. It's at those times that personal resonance must kick in and help all parties through the crisis. It is a lot easier to work with people you like in times of crisis. Trust will carry the management/coach relationship during normal times; trust and friendship will carry the relationship better when times are tough.

Notes

1. While the focus of this chapter is team building, it is not meant to address every kind of potential teammate. As such, certain potential team members are not discussed here; this is not meant to suggest that they are unimportant.
2. There has been a proliferation of family types in the United States in recent years. For a fascinating overview of these variations, see Nathan Yau, "Most Common Family Types in America," FlowingData.com, and David H. Lenck, "The 50 Most Common Family Types in America," *Wealthmanagement.com*, July 20, 2016.

3.   Shelly Schwartz, "Wealthy Suffer from 'Estate-Planning Fatigue,'" CNBC, June 29, 2015. This article describes the ebbs and flows of recent tax law changes. However, the changes referenced in this article don't account for the fact that nearly 40 percent of Americans with $1 million or more have done *no estate planning at all!*

4.   The argument for avoiding the do-it-yourself route is straightforward: It's too easy and too costly to make a mistake. For examples, see Gary Flotron and Randy Whitelaw, "A Comprehensive Perspective on the Four UPIA-TOLI Cases, Plus One That Includes the UTC, and Their Astounding Implications for ILIT Trustees," *Steve Leimberg's Estate Planning Newsletter*, July 20, 2016; David J. Yvars Sr., "Ten Mistakes to Avoid in Managing Assets for Estates," *Trust & Estates*, May 31, 2016; and "Estate's Administrators Were Liable for Decedent's Unpaid Income Taxes," *Checkpoint Newsstand*, March 21, 2014. Another reason for avoiding the DIY approach is scams; see Steve Leimberg, "The 'Dirty Dozen'— IRS Notes Tax Scams That Cost All of Us Millions," *Steve Leimberg's Income Tax Planning Newsletter*, April 13, 2016. An aid to the one-man approach, at least in terms of investing, is the advance of the robo-advisor; see Ross Kerber, "Meet Your Financial Advisor, the Cyborg," *Reuters*, June 17, 2016. Another is just following good basic advice; see "Why You Should Start Investing and the Three Golden Rules to Make It Work," *Daily Mail*, March 25, 2014. Also, for wealth transfer and distribution planning basics, see "Estate Planning Checklist: How to Communicate Your Wishes," *Premier Trust*, December 2015 and Russ Alan Prince, "The Whole Client Model," *Private Wealth*, February 14, 2014.

5.   How does "big money" handle its needs? They use advisors; see, "The Ultra Rich Listen to Financial Advisors," *Wealthmanagement.com*, April 8, 2016.

6.   To appreciate the depth and breadth of knowledge necessary to successfully manage wealth transfer and distribution, see Steve Akers, "2016 Heckerling Musings," *Steve Leimberg's Estate Planning Newsletter*, March 31, 2016. Steve's "Heckerling Nuggets" provide a detailed annual review of what's happening in the game of Wealth Transfer and Distribution. One quick review should convince most readers that our game is not for the faint of heart! While a quick read might discourage some players, you can come to understand the need for help just as well from a short article; see Dan Caplinger, "What Wealth Management IS (and What It Should Be)," *The Motley Fool*, February 22, 2016. For another overview, see the Notre Dame Tax and Estate Planning Institute, another annual program: https://notredame-web.ungerboeck.com/coe/coe_p2_details. aspx?eventid=18076&sessionid=fd0fa3fboeioeikej6.

7.   One topic that has begun to attract more attention—and rightly so—is the role of women in wealth transfer and distribution. Women in the United States today control more wealth than men, and are expected to see their share grow over time; for more information, see Ryan Gorman, "Women Now Control More than Half of US Personal Wealth, Which Will Only Increase in Years to Come," *Business Insider*, April 7, 2015. Second, women are often treated inappropriately when it comes wealth transfer and distribution; for more information, see Thomas Seubert, "Everything the Financial Services Industry Knows About Women Is Wrong," *Wealthmanagement.com*, August 17, 2016; "What You're Really Thinking: Understanding the Financial Lives of Women," a research study by United Capital Financial Life Management, August 2016; and "Men Think Differently about Their Futures as Women Take 40% of B School Seats," *Bloomberg News*, November 9, 2015.

8.   Robert Laura, "Traditional Retirement Planning for Couples Is Fatally Flawed," *Forbes*, August 10, 2016.

9.   "The Golden Rule of Estate Planning: Your Spouse Comes First," insurancenewsnet.com, May 4, 2015.

10. Some of the best examples come from the results of disharmony; see Michael Fischer, "Making Sure Your Client's Estate Doesn't Go 'Redstone,'" *Private Wealth*, June 20, 2016.

11. On-field manager is a position that stimulates competition. There are usually several candidates, and each can make his or her own case. To study the argument for hiring a Chartered Financial Consultant® to be your manager, see "How and Why You Should Manage Your Client's Team," Blog of the American College of Financial Services, August 5, 2016.

12. One of the characteristics of wealth transfer and distribution is its dynamic nature. For recent changes to the dynamic, see "HNWI's Vision for Wealth Management in the Information Age," *FactSet*, August 2016, and Greg King, "Four Emerging HNWI Expectations Wealth Mangers Must Meet," *Trust Advisor*, August 7, 2016. For legal changes, see Carly E. Howard and Michael Sneeringer, "Fiduciary Law Trends," *Trust & Estates*, May 2016, pages 56–59. Also see Amelia Renkert-Thomas, "The Trustee's Role in an Owner's Council," *Trusts & Estates*, May 2016, pages 52–55.

13. Mark Hurley, "How 'Best Wealth Manager' Lists Mislead You," MarketWatch.com, September 30, 2014. High-profile firms can be as interested in their own welfare as that of the client; see Olivia Oran, "Morgan Stanley Wants 'More Wallet from Clients,'" *Reuters*, June 15, 2016. Also see Tara Siegel Bernard, "More Protection for a Nest Egg Has Some Brokers Upset," *New York Times*, September 18, 2015. On the importance of vetting, see Paul Sullivan, "Deciding if a Financial Adviser Is Right for the Job," *New York Times*, June 20, 2016, and Matt Oechsli, "Thirteen True Differentiators for Financial Advisors," *Wealthmanagement.com*, June 2, 2016. For vetting estate attorneys, see Kim Kamin, "10 Questions Advisors Should Ask When Hiring an Estate Planning Attorney," *Wealthmanagement.com*, May 5, 2016. For evidence that accounting firms are lagging in this area, see Russ Alan Prince, "Why Small Accounting Firms Are Missing the Wealth Management Opportunity," *Forbes*, December 2, 2015. For banks, see Russ Alan Prince, "Providing Wealth Management Services to Middle-Market Commercial Banking Clients," *Forbes*, July 29, 2015. Equally faulty decisions can result from the selection of someone ill-prepared to accept the role and its responsibilities; see Patricia Angus, "After the Plan," *Trust & Estates*, May 12, 2016. There is help available for the novice, however; see Christopher Holtby, "A Helpline for Family of Friends as Trustees Balance Obligations without Ceding Control," *Trust Advisor*, January 12, 2016. There is also an argument to be made for corporate trustees; see "Hazards of Depending on an Individual Trustee," *Counsel Trust*, 2015.

14. For a study that carefully and thoroughly examines the client/advisor relationship, especially as applies to investments, see "Understanding Today's Affluent," a report by First Clearing and The Oechsli Institute, November 2015. Protecting the rights of the owner and the family are paramount in our game. The seriousness of this position needs little confirmation; see Keith A. Davidson, "When You Must Sue: Trustees' Duty to Enforce Claims," *Wealthmanagement.com*, May 27, 2016.

15. Todd Fithian, Albert E. Gibbons, and David W. Holaday, "High Performance Teaming and Professional Collaboration," *Trusts & Estates*, May 2016, pages 22–30.

16. David H. Lenok, "Wealth Managers Should Mind the Digital Gap," *Wealthmanagement.com*, May 31, 2016.

17. Brian Broderick, "The Wealth-Transfer 'Talk'" *Private Wealth*, July 10, 2015.

18. Jennifer Pendergast, "Grooming New Leaders," *Private Wealth*, September 9, 2015.

19. One of the more important recent developments in estate planning has been the use of Trust Protectors; for a good and quick overview, see Matthew T. McClintock, "Thinking Deeper about Protectors and Their Powers," *Steve Leimberg's Estate Planning Newsletter*, July 21, 2016. Similarly, there is an increasing role for fiduciaries; see Alexander A. Bove Jr., "To Be or Not to Be—A Fiduciary, That Is," *Steve Leimberg's Estate Planning Newsletter*, June 30, 2016; Alexander A. Bove Jr., "Conquering the Fear of Fiduciary Duty," *Trusts & Estates*,

May 2016, pages 60–62. Also see Ryan W. Smith, "Breaking Down the Fiduciary Rule, Parts One through Five," DOL Fiduciary Rule, May 23–25, 2016.

20. David H. Lenok, "Wealth Managers Should Mind the Digital Gap," *Wealthmanagement. com*, May 31, 2016.

21. Russ Alan Prince, "The Tax Buster," *Private Wealth*, July 2015. For a convincing argument on the need for coaches and specialists, even with a single discipline, see Craig R. Hersch, "Building an Estate-Planning Team," *Trusts & Estates*, May 3, 2016.

22. Even medical specialists can have a role in wealth transfer and distribution; see "UBS Recommends WorldClinic to HNW Clients," *Private Wealth*, June 16, 2015. Similarly, there are specialists in working with children of wealthy families; see "Inheritance Prep for Wealthy Kids Seen as Niche Market," *Reuters*, March 6, 2015.

Chapter 6

Keeping Score

————————◆————————

Prologue

Scorekeeping is personal; it's based on an individual's goals and objectives and on what assets are in play. It also means something different to every person. Success is measured by whether you achieve your objectives, and at what costs. For example, a distribution that delivers ninety cents on the dollar might seem successful unless you know that it would have been easy to deliver every dollar without cost. On the other hand, someone else might deliver 75 percent of her assets, and this might seem low until you consider that the norm is 50 percent. In still other cases, success is measured by a sense of well-being and accomplishment as opposed to monetary measures. Each of us needs to arrive at a definition of success based on our understanding of what's possible and what we value.

In 1999 one of my favorite clients, Jim, was unexpectedly and tragically diagnosed with a disease that would take his life within a year. Up to that point, Jim had always taken a long-term view of his goals. More than anything else, he was devoted to his family and wanted them to enjoy as fully as possible the legacy he had worked so hard to leave them.[1] He had accumulated his wealth through hard work, starting with virtually nothing and building a successful company at a young age. And when the time was right, he sold that company. He identified and adjusted his objectives as he went along, and modified his support system as necessary.

Jim and I started working together in the mid 1980s. At that time he was very young—in his mid thirties—and had just bought the company where he'd worked for the past few years. Over the next ten years his net worth blossomed as the company grew significantly in value. Despite Jim's youth, we made sure from the beginning of our relationship that he and his family were prepared to deal with potential tax issues. One of his goals was to buffer his estate against death taxes—in the late '80s and early '90s, personal assets were subject to estate taxes on as little as $1 million.[2] Jim's net worth was significantly higher, so he wanted strategies that mitigated or even eliminated taxes. Since we knew that his goal was to deliver what he had to his family with as little dilution as possible, we needed to think outside the box.

To meet his asset-protection goals, Jim established an irrevocable trust and used cash gifts to fund it with life insurance. An irrevocable trust is a trust that normally cannot be modified once put in place. By establishing such a trust, the grantor effectively surrenders his or her ownership of the assets within. For this reason, when properly formed and funded, irrevocable trusts can serve as tax shelters with enormous capacity. In Jim's case, the goal was to use small amounts of hard dollars (annual cash gifts) to generate large amounts of soft dollars (life insurance proceeds), which would subsequently be available to the estate for transfer costs.[3] Of course, when we created this trust, we never anticipated that we would need the funds as soon as we did.

By the mid-1990s Jim had decided that the time was right to sell the business (a challenge I described briefly when I first mentioned him in chapter 3). He had grown the business into a regional company, and his prospective buyers included a number of public companies. When it came time to sell, Jim looked for ways to mitigate the tax cost of the sale, and together we found a way to defer taxes. As I recounted in chapter 3, we decided to turn down a cash sale and instead take his payout in the form of stock in the acquiring company, an approach known as a *stock-for-stock exchange*. Jim was very comfortable with the buying company's prospects and was more than happy to own their stock. By doing this, he managed to delay millions in capital gains taxes.

After this sale, Jim revisited his financial situation and concluded that our earlier planning needed further enhancement. Since his net worth had increased dramatically with the growth and sale of his company, Jim decided to add more life insurance to his irrevocable trust. This required increased gifts to the trust, which then allowed him to leverage these funds into additional coverage. Because we used this combination of an irrevocable trust, lifetime gifting, and life insurance to its fullest advantage, the trust's assets were positioned to avoid estate, gift, or income taxes and maximize the funds available in case of his death.[4]

This updated transfer plan anticipated any and all death taxes. Because his planning had kept up with his needs, when Jim learned that his life was in danger, he was able to address his health issues without worrying about what problems he would leave his family. In the last few months of Jim's life, he and I met several times to make sure that his objectives were met, and every meeting confirmed that his plans were going to work. Since we knew Jim was financially sound, he was able to devote his final months to his wife and children rather than to the impossible task of seeing to their welfare at the last minute.[5]

Unfortunately, Jim died too early. By determining how he was going to "keep score," however—that is, by clearly outlining his objectives and measuring the effects of his actions on those objectives—he delivered his entire estate intact to his wife and children. Death costs could have shrunk his estate by more than $10 million, but we managed those costs with the insurance that Jim had acquired and maintained, and we delivered the entire estate without dilution by substituting insurance proceeds for hard assets.

Keeping score is necessary in the game of Wealth Transfer and Distribution. Jim's objectives required a degree of planning that far exceeded what most people would ever need to contemplate, but together we were able to create a plan that delivered everything he had to his family, which makes clear that no one need ever assume that any goal is impossible.

Everyone keeps score differently, and the metrics we use for scorekeeping depend on what is available for transfer and distribution and on our individual objectives. For example, suppose your basketball team is ahead by twenty points with only five minutes left in the game; both of these facts—the actual score and the time remaining on the clock—will affect the coach's decision making. Can you afford to take risks? Do you *need* to take risks? The team that is twenty points behind will answer these questions very differently than your team will. Your team may want simply to play defensively and hold onto your lead for the next five minutes, whereas the other team will need to concentrate all its energy on strong offensive play if they hope to erase your lead. This is the essence of scorekeeping. By clearly establishing goals and objectives and then monitoring the results of our efforts as time goes by—measuring results against expectations and adjusting goals and tactics as necessary—we can increase the probability of getting what we have to whom we want, when we want, how we want.

———————— ◆ ————————

We're all born broke. Some of us have well-to-do parents who enrich us, but no baby ever came out of the womb with a job. If our parents aren't wealthy, we have to go out and earn a living when we grow up. And how do we keep score?[6] By accumulating things, and by spending less than we make so that we can save something.[7] And by occasionally buying nice things for ourselves when we feel that we've moved up in the world.

Savings is part of keeping score, and so is moving up. When we move up, we may not have more money to show for it, but hopefully, we have a nicer lifestyle. This is how some people keep score: They buy a better car. They live in a better neighborhood. Other people say, "I don't want to have stuff. I would rather take my excess funds and save them. Rather than a seventy-inch flat-screen TV, I'm going to buy a forty-inch TV and put that $300 difference in my pocket. I won't spend all the money I've got."[8]

For Jim, keeping score was both monetary and psychological; he wanted to make sure that whatever he had left would benefit his wife and his children. He didn't want his family to be forced to liquidate $8 million in hard assets in order to pay transfer taxes on their $20 million inheritance. At the same time, he wanted them to respect and love one another; he didn't want them to argue about money. Jim kept score by thinking at all times, *How do I protect myself, and how do I protect the people I love?* And when his score suddenly and catastrophically changed, he was prepared.[9]

Nothing Is Easy—the Elusiveness of True Efficiency

Every game keeps score in one way or another. Scorekeeping can be simple or complicated, but it is the process of determining whether the goal or objective has been met. In figure skating and diving, for example, there are two aspects to the score: the performance itself—that is, technical considerations of proper form and technique—and the degree of artistic expression employed in the act. Both are measured, and points are awarded or deducted for each aspect.

It's much the same in the game of Wealth Transfer and Distribution. There are two metrics used for keeping score in our game: effectiveness and efficiency. Effectiveness is the simpler concept; it amounts to getting done what we want done—accomplishing our goal. Efficiency, on the other hand, is a very different concept. Accomplishing a goal *efficiently* means getting it done with the fewest deviations from our expected route. In golf, for example, a hole-in-one is the most efficient result. Unfortunately, in Wealth Transfer as in golf, holes-in-one are rare.

To be sure, *relative* efficiency—i.e., successful wealth transfer with minimal tax loss—is not uncommon in our game. When we find *true* efficiency in our game, however, it is usually on the side of Wealth Distribution, in situations in which one person passes value to another person without any of it being lost to taxation. True efficiency in wealth transfer situations is rare outside of simple transactions. In most cases, the best we can hope for is the most efficient approach possible rather than true efficiency.[10]

Making a wealth transfer in any other medium besides cash almost always reduces efficiency. For me to give you $14,000 in cash costs neither of us a dime in tax. But what if I want to give you my stamp collection? The collection may be worth only $3,000—a far cry from the $14,000 limit we've been discussing throughout this book—but the act of monetization (i.e., selling the stamp collection), will, in most cases, precipitate a taxable event. Even trading some of the stamps with another collector, or trading the entire collection for something of more interest to you—comic books, motorcycle parts, or whatever you're interested in—may have tax consequences.

That's not to say that there's never a reason to make or accept such a gift. If I'm in a higher tax bracket than you are, monetizing the stamp collection will cost me more than it would cost you . . . possibly a lot more. Therefore, less value will be lost in the transfer if you sell the collection after you receive it than if I were to sell it and give you the money.

How are effectiveness and efficiency relevant to scorekeeping? These concepts are important because every player needs to know that distributions and transfers are not apt to be easy. Many of my clients start playing the game with the assumption that what they want done is easy. In other words, scoring is almost taken for granted. After all, how hard can it be to move wealth from one person to another? In fact, it can be very difficult . . . and almost impossible if the goal is to pass along significant wealth without dilution. None of this should discourage anyone from playing the game, but it should serve as a caution; an apparently simple objective may not be as easy as it seems. Holes in one, grand slams, series sweeps, and championships are admired precisely because they are hard to accomplish, requiring both effectiveness and efficiency.

As I said before, many players fail to understand the game, and try to score without being conscious of what is involved. It's harder than it looks. While they may succeed to some extent, their success probably will be limited, and what success they do enjoy will likely come by accident—the equivalent of guessing correctly in a game of heads or tails. As the goal of transfer or distribution becomes larger in terms of value, more complicated in terms of assets, or more demanding in terms of tax treatment, the heads-or-tails approach starts to work against the player as the odds get longer and luck becomes more elusive. To play the game of Wealth Transfer and Distribution well, it is essential to identify the measure of scoring: whom we wish to receive what, when, and under what circumstances. This is much more complicated than calling heads or tails, but it is how score is really kept.

Winter Rules

Since each transaction is different, each player determines a winning score differently. Even in situations in which people look to be doing the same thing, there can be differences based on the smallest consideration. Take Bob and Mike, two fathers who each want to gift $20,000 to their children. Bob is married, whereas Mike is divorced—a fact that makes Mike's goal more complicated and difficult than Bob's. Bob can simply write a check (regardless of whether the account is shared by his wife, Ann) and call it a day because Bob's and Ann's respective $14,000 gift allowances add up to $28,000—more than enough to cover the $20,000 gift Bob wants to make.

Mike, on the other hand, has a problem because his goal exceeds the $14,000-per-year per recipient that the law allows as a gift. Both dads want the same thing, and both have the money. But Bob can complete his gift in ten minutes, whereas Mike needs to consult with one of his coaches. Should it be this difficult? No. *Is* this difficult? Obviously. To make matters worse, Mike may be unaware that this distribution carries transfer issues if he does the wrong thing (this happens every day). Could Mike inadvertently create problems for himself? The answer to that question is ambiguous, so for now we'll just say *maybe*.

This example reminds us of what we learned in chapters 3 and 4: Sometimes rules are elastic if you know how to use them. In golf, there is a well-known tradition from late fall until mid-spring: winter rules. Because course conditions may not be as uniform as at other times of year, regular rules are suspended and players are allowed to reset their balls before hitting. In golf this process of improving your lie amounts to a forgiveness program. The same concession is available in our game of Wealth Transfer.

Going back to Mike and his gifts, Mike wanted to give $20,000 to his son, but was prevented from doing so by the $14,000 limit. His goal was out of reach by $6,000. However, in Wealth Transfer there is an element of winter rules. If Mike knows this, he can reach his goal and give $20,000 to his child despite not having the same freedom Bob had by simply being married; he can move the ball around. He can find other allowances—other liberties that he's allowed—and move those assets over to increase what he's allowed to give his child. He can do this by making use of his Lifetime Exemption Allowance (which you'll recall we discussed in chapter 3) and filing what's known as a *gift-tax return*.[11] In brief, a gift-tax return is required when the player exceeds his $14,000 Annual Exclusion limit to anyone in a given year. Mike exceeded his limit by gifting $20,000 and was required to file a gift-tax return to capture these excess gifts in an aggregated running tally. If Mike made excess gifts of $6,000 for two years, his Lifetime Exemption would decrease by $12,000. There would be no tax; just an informational return.

By taking advantage of the IRS's "winter rules" in this way, Mike keeps score. He is paying attention to his options in the context of the assets he owns, what he wants to do with them, and his understanding of the rules (a subject that you'll recall we discussed in chapter 3). Securing Mike's goal—i.e., scoring—is made possible by understanding that sometimes there are special circumstances that allow us to do more than we thought we could. Is Mike's result as effective as Bob's? Yes, but only because he used a concession that the rule book allows. Is it as efficient? Unfortunately, no. In order to score, Mike had to make a sacrifice (in the form of the early use of some of his Lifetime Exemption, as described above) but that sacrifice was worth the cost.[12]

The Significance of the Environment

By now, one thing should be clear: Part of the game—what I consider to be the beauty of the game—is that distributions and transfers are as varied as the people making them. As a result, everyone plays the game differently. Although the scores at the end of play may be the same for Mike and Bob (both managed to gift $20,000), they achieved their scores in different ways. The difference between the two cases is the circumstances under which the distributions were accomplished. In Bob's case, the transfer was easy, with no wasted motion. In Mike's case, the distribution was more difficult because he had one more step to complete. Unfortunately—and I have seen this happen many times—Mike might have never realized that there was an extra step if his on-field manager hadn't spotted the need for him to file a gift-tax return.

Players must recognize that every transaction is unique because who receives what varies from case to case. This means that unconscious actions (meaning, in Mike's case, failure to be conscious of one's options and obligations) can lead to unintended consequences. For this reason, it helps to understand the environment in which your game is being played.

Environments are important in most games. In competitive team sports, at almost every level of play, there is a home-field advantage. The Boston Celtics had a distinct advantage for years because of their unique parquet floor; other teams only played at Boston Garden a few times a year, while the Celtics practiced and played there daily and knew the dead spots from the more lively spots. The swirling winds of Candlestick Park gave the 49ers unique kicking advantages because they were familiar with how those winds blew. In a more pedestrian sport, my Ping-Pong table favors me over you because I understand the playing environment better than you do.

Environment is therefore a broader concept than the *playing field* we discussed in chapter 4 (although the concept of environment certainly encompasses the playing field, among other things). For example, my Ping-Pong table is itself the playing field, and my unique familiarity with its shape, contours, and surface imperfections is part of the reason for the advantage it provides me. But there are other factors to consider: the lighting in the basement where the table is kept, the potentially distracting echoes of the sound of play due to the acoustics of the room, the draft from an improperly sealed window on one side of the table. These *environmental* factors, together with the field of play represented by the table itself, must be accounted for by anyone who hopes to beat me at this game.

In wealth transfer and distribution, players must consider several materially different environments: tax laws, legal cases and their interpretations, legislative actions, economic conditions, cultural mores, and other outside influences.[13] Each of these deserves attention because each affects how the game is played and influences whether the player scores. These environments have a broader impact beyond effectiveness (scoring), however; they also affect efficiency (at what cost points are scored). In simple distributions like those that Bob and Mike made, the effect of external influences on environments generally will be limited (although we saw that Mike had to account for tax laws to effect his result). As distributions and transfers become more complicated, however, the likelihood of environmental impacts grows.[14]

Matters are further complicated by the fact that that these environments are dynamic; they change, and change often. Sometimes the change can be abrupt and jarring; other times it can be slow and less impactful. Either way, the fact that the environments change as they do adds another layer of complexity to game playing. An example of this in occurred in 2010, when estate taxes were suspended for one year. Unmarried individuals who died in 2010 escaped a 50 percent tax on cumulative personal assets in excess of $3 million. This was, in a way, a simple case of being in the right place at the right time—dying under the right circumstances. While the personal cost—death—was high, the transfer cost for individuals who died that year was low, and potentially nothing. The difference between dying on December 31, 2009, and January 1, 2010, was potentially worth millions. Don't think for a minute that many families in late 2009 didn't actively look for ways to prolong life for a few days more!

———————— ♦ ————————

In wealth transfer, success is measured by the player's ability to look back and say, "This worked as I hoped it would" (or even better). Players who overlook environment or fail to define success experience disappointing results, and this happens more often than successful outcomes. These families find that their outcomes were more expensive, complicated, frustrating, or time-consuming than they had planned.

The difference between failure and success is not as great as many people think, however. It can be like hitting a home run and failing to touch one of the bases; the player may have taken all the right actions and neglected a minor point. This is how even the best teams can snatch defeat from the jaws of victory.

Notes

1. Making a transfer and distribution in no way ensures that the recipients will do right by their gift; see Scott Martin, "Easy Come, Easy Go: Why 35% of Americans Squander Their Inheritance," *Trust Advisor*, November 18, 2015. Creating and leaving legacies in the United States is significantly different than in Europe; see Alessandro Speciale and Chiara Vassari, "How to Stay Rich in Europe: Inherit Money for 700 Years," *Bloomberg*, August 24, 2016. The definition of wealth also varies from place to place, even in the United States; see "The View from San Francisco Bay Area," *Charles Schwab*, April 2016. In this study, respondents suggest that it requires twice the amount to be "wealthy" in San Francisco as elsewhere in the US. Also see John J. Bowen Jr. et al., *The State of the Affluent 2014*, CEG Worldwide.
2. For a short and readable overview of the Estate Tax in the United States, see Patricia M. Soldano and Michael Palicz, "A Historic Overview of Legislation," *Trusts & Estates*, September 2016, pages 49–51.
3. For an overview of the uses of irrevocable trusts funded with life insurance, see "Irrevocable Life Insurance Trust (ILIT)," *The Wealth Counselor LLC*.
4. Since Jim passed away, newer approaches have been developed to protect assets; see Rachel Podnos, "Your Revocable Trust Is Not Protecting Your Assets," *Nasdaq*, July 5, 2016.
5. Family interaction is much overlooked in the process of wealth transfer and distribution. We often neglect to discuss how what we have is to be transferred and distributed. Rather than being candid, many families avoid "the money talk" as much as possible. See Bruce S. Udell, "How to Help Your Children Financially Now Without Giving Them Any Money," *Kiplinger Wealth Creation*, July 2016. Even advisors are sometimes reticent to have "the talk"; see Ken Nopar, "The Benefits of the Charitable Giving Talk," *Financial Advisor*, May 29, 2015. Despite their reticence to discuss financial matters, worries about money keep Americans awake at night; see Chuck Jaffe, "Americans Worry More About Their Finances than Anything Else," *MarketWatch*, September 15, 2015. For the benefits of openness, see Robert Laura, "Three Pillars of Peace of Mind in Retirement," *Financial Advisor*, March 13, 2015.
6. Getting our arms around what we own is critical; after all, until we know what we have, we really can't determine what we are going to do with it. For a current view of net worth in the United States, see Doug Short, "Household Net Worth: The Real Story," *Advisor*

Perspectives, June 9, 2016. There is serious wealth inequality in the United States, which can discourage people from trying to accumulate; see Jeanne Sahadi, "The Richest 10% Hold 76% of the Wealth," *CNN Money*, August 18, 2016. Also see Thomas Seubert, "Millennials Don't Think They Can Save $1 Million for Retirement," *WealthManagement.com*, August 3, 2016, and Rich Miller, "Wealth Bubble in 'Scary Graph' Flashes Warning about Future U.S. Downturn," *Bloomberg*, July 22, 2016. The same is true for income; see John Mauldin, "The Trouble with Trade," *Thoughts from the Frontline*, July 31, 2016. This problem is not limited to the United States; the United Kingdom faces the same difficulty. See Laura Gardiner, "Stagnation Generation: the Case for Renewing the Intergenerational Contract," *Resolution Foundation*, July 18, 2016. Retirement savings are also in crisis; see Nari Rhee, "The Retirement Savings Crisis," *National Institute on Retirement Security*, June 2013. It is reasonable to ask whether successful people share certain characteristics; for one man's opinion, see Mark Ford, "9 Wealth-Creating Lessons I've Learned from Billionaires," *The Crux*, August 4, 2015.

7. Managing debt is critical to wealth creation. For current information on household debt in America, see John Mauldin, "Life on the Edge," *Thoughts from the Frontline*, May 14, 2016; Gary Halbert, "Fed: Almost Half of US Households Have Under $400 Saved," *Forecasts & Trends*, May 31, 2016; Gary Halbert, "Average Household Debt: $132,000—Not Counting Mortgage," *Advisor Perspectives*, August 31, 2016; and Tony Sagami, "The Trillion-Dollar Investment Opportunity," *Connecting the Dots*, June 14, 2016. Spending is a two-edged sword; on the one hand, it implies prosperity, while on the other, it can create debt. See John V. Duca, Anthony Murphy, and Elizabeth Organ, "Increased Credit Availability, Rising Asset Prices Help Boost Consumer Spending," *Dallas Fed*, April 2016.

8. As part of the game of Wealth Transfer and Distribution, account holders must make use of their retirement savings during their lives; for an overview, see Suzanne Woolley, "Boomers, It's Time to Spend—and Pay Taxes on—Your 401(k)," *Bloomberg*, June 27, 2016, and Mark Miller, "Solving the Retirement Withdrawal Equation," *WealthManagement Magazine*, June 15, 2016. One of the approaches that I believe makes the most sense for long-term wealth accumulation is acquiring dividend-paying stocks with two characteristics: increased dividends on a yearly basis and overall business growth. For a brief introduction to the idea, see Tony Sagami, "Dividends and Prosperity," *Connecting the Dots*, August 9, 2016. For more information on this approach, see "September 2016 List of Dividends Aristocrats," *Sure Dividend*, September 1, 2016. Chuck Carnevale provides a wealth of information and analysis on high-quality, fairly valued dividend stocks; for examples of his work, see Chuck Carnevale, "Premier Dividend Growth Stocks: Is There Any Value? A Sector by Sector Summary—Part I," *Seeking Alpha*, August 22, 2016, and "A Comprehensive Look at Dividend Growth Stock Valuations Sector by Sector: Part 2," *Advisor Perspectives*, August 28, 2016. Another major source of good information is The Dividend Guy; see The Dividend Guy, "What are Dividend Kings?" *Dividend Stocks Rock*, August 26, 2016; "6 Investment Tips for Small Portfolio," *The Dividend Guy Blog*, August 8, 2016; and "Key Metrics for Dividend Growth Investors," *Dividend Stocks Rock*, August 7, 2106.

9. Keeping score can also include avoiding problems and headaches; see "The Rich Worry More about Identity Theft than Terrorism," *WealthManagement.com*, September 1, 2016. At the same time, it can raise personal anxieties; see "Seven Psychological Issues for Clients Making Bequests," *Idea Xchange*, August 2, 2016. In times of volatility, planning tools can be flawed; see Lance Roberts, "Why the Next Decade Will Foil Financial Plans," *Advisor Perspectives*, June 13, 2016. Also see Evan Simonoff, "Why Clients Fail at Retirement," *Financial Advisor*, June 2013.

10. Since most Americans are highly dependent on Social Security as a source of retirement income, it offers an excellent laboratory for viewing effectiveness and efficiency at work. See

John Mauldin, "Maximizing Your Social Security Benefits," *Outside the Box*, June 1, 2016. For a more in-depth look, see Lawrence J. Kotlikoff, Philip Moeller, and Paul Solman, *Get What's Yours: The Secrets to Maxing Out Your Social Security* (New York, Simon & Schuster, 2016).

11. For a simple explanation of gift strategies exceeding the Annual Exclusion amount, see Julie Garber, "Gift Tax Exclusion: Annual Exclusion vs. Lifetime Exemption," *The Balance*, April 26, 2015; Ashlea Ebeling, "IRS Announces 2016 Estate and Gift Tax Limits: The $10.9 Million Tax Break," *Forbes,* October 22, 2015; and Matthew Frankel, "Use the 2016 Gift Tax Exclusion to Beat the Estate Tax," *The Motley Fool,* January 12, 2016. For a more refined and comprehensive explanation, consult a qualified tax attorney, an estate-planning attorney, or a CPA with a master's degree in taxation.

12. Bruce Helmer and Peg Webb, "Commentary: When Does It Make Sense to Add a Trust to Your Estate Plan?" *Brainerd Dispatch*, July 23, 2016.

13. Many things contribute to changes in environment. For demographic impact, see Matthew Tracey and Joachim Fels, "70 Is the New 65: Demographics Still Support 'Lower Rates for Longer,'" *PIMCO.com,* February 2016, and Michael Avery and Philip Sanders, "Millennials Lead: Today's Largest Generation Will Impact U.S. Economy and Markets," *Advisor Perspectives*, July 10, 2015. For a quick guide to assets in rank of ownership preference, see William Baldwin, "Estate Planning: A Ranking of Good Assets and Bad Assets," *Forbes,* August 25, 2014. For how the wealth industry is changing, see Michael Raneri, "7 Ways Wealth Management Client Attitudes Are Shifting," *Forbes,* May 12, 2015. For a brief overview on the effect of divorce, see Deborah Nason, "Getting Remarried? Protect Your Assets and Your Interests," *CNBC,* July 28, 2016; for a scholarly overview, see Jeff Scroggin, "Tax, Estate, and Practical Issues in Divorce and Remarriage," *Steve Leimberg's Estate Planning Email Newsletter*, August 3, 2015. For the effects of a spousal death, see Aaron Katsman, "Money Mistakes to Avoid After a Spouse's Death," *MoneyWatch,* September 4, 2015. For tax/legislative changes, see Jonathan G. Blattmachr and Mitchell M. Gans, "Treasury Issues Broad Section 2704 Regulations," *Trusts & Estates*, August 3, 2016; John M. Goralka and Jim Magner, "The Credit Shelter/Bypass Trust—An Estate Tax Time Bomb," *Steve Leimberg's Estate Planning E-mail Newsletter*, May 2, 2016; and Blanche Lark Christerson, "The President's FY 2017 Tax Proposals," *Deutsche Bank Tax Topics*, February, 24, 2016. For the effect of technology, see Christopher Steele, "Creating an Effective Digital Estate Plan," *WealthManagement.com*, July 20, 2016 and Gregory Bresiger, "Millennials Are Ditching Financial Advisors for Apps," *New York Post,* July 10, 2016. For the effect of record-low interest rates, see Justin Splitter, "This 5,000-Year Low Is Ruining Your Retirement," *Casey Daily Dispatch*, July 2016. For the effect of "death taxes," see Matt McClintock, "Nobody Pays Estate Tax Anymore . . . but Almost Everyone Has a 'Death Tax' Problem," *Steve Leimberg's Estate Planning E-mail Newsletter*, June 20, 2016.

14. James Picerno, "How 'Safe' Are Rich Retirees?" *Private Wealth Magazine*, Spring 2016, pages 33–35. A new law passed in late 2015 changed the landscape for basis accounting. This law was designed to preclude a beneficiary from using a more favorable fair-market value for an asset than could be had using estate tax value. See Hannah Mensch and Stacey Delich-Gould, "Treasury's Consistent Basis Regulations—A Primer" *Steve Leimberg's Estate Planning E-mail Newsletter*, March 9, 2016.

Chapter 7

Playing Defense

— ◆ —

Prologue

Making sure that our efforts achieve our goals is critical in the game of Wealth Transfer and Distribution; no one wants to expend time and money only to fail. For this reason, playing defense is one of the keystones of success. It is necessary to think defensively in order to ensure that our careful planning produces the intended result, to anticipate and prepare for unexpected catastrophes, and to change our course when we see something going in the wrong direction. Playing defense takes many forms, some simple and some complex, and these forms can be best illustrated with a series of examples:

Margie decides to send $100 checks to each of five charities. Four of these charities respond quickly by sending her letters of gratitude and receipts for her donations. The fifth charity doesn't respond with any acknowledgment or receipt. Margie knows that deducting her gifts for tax purposes requires a receipt from the charity. It isn't enough to have a record of the donation, or even her cancelled check. To be protected, she needs formal acknowledgment. Accordingly, she calls the charity to make sure that she gets the necessary receipt.[1]

Eric wants to help his three grandchildren with their college costs. He knows that he can fund a 529 plan (which is essentially a tax shelter designed for funds that have been earmarked for college education), but he wants to make a larger gift than $14,000 to each grandchild and isn't quite sure how to do it. He asks his accountant, Ralph, how to make two years' gifts at once. Ralph tells Eric that he can donate $28,000 to each grandchild in year one by using the 529 plan to "frontload" two years' worth of gifts into a single year. Once he does this, however, he won't be able to make any other gifts to these grandchildren for the next two years without exceeding his annual gifting allowance.[2] To make sure that Eric remembers this, Ralph takes the extra step of sending Eric reminders around the Christmas holidays and the grandchildren's birthdays to avoid additional gifts. Finally, after two years have passed, Ralph sends Eric one more note, advising him that he can once again make gifts to his grandchildren if he wants.

Delores is a widow who has always been very independent, but she is now concerned that if she were to fall seriously ill, no one would know how to help her. She decides to review her financial relationship with Hal, who has been her financial advisor for years, and give him her financial power of attorney.[3] Delores entrusts Hal with this power in order to ensure that, should she ever become incapacitated by accident or sudden illness, there would be no disruption to her lifestyle or to Hal's ability to act on her behalf. While she is healthy, however, Delores retains absolute authority over her financial affairs; Hal's assumption of this power would be triggered only by Delores's incapacity (for example, if she were to sustain a head injury and fall into a coma).[4]

However, Delores wants to add another layer of protection. Besides knowing how she pays her bills and where her Social Security check is deposited, she wants Hal to be able to access her safe-deposit box. To this end, Delores gives him signatory authority on the box today.[5] Hal understands the gravity of Delores's actions; he can now access her most private property. As additional protection for both Delores and himself, he decides to get a fiduciary liability policy to insure himself against claims if something were to go wrong. In doing so, Hal is also playing defense, but in a different way.

Delores's actions, while necessary for her protection, create an additional level of complexity. She is therefore fortunate to have a competent financial advisor like Hal to guide her through the process of erecting defenses against any possible calamity.[6]

John and Sue have a daughter, Chris, who has just turned sixteen. Chris wants to get her driver's license as soon as possible, and has saved money for her own car. While John and Sue understand her wishes, they are concerned about increased liability exposure. Chris is very responsible, but teenage drivers as a group are a higher-risk insurance category. To make sure they do everything possible to prepare Chris for driving, her parents have her attend and pass a driver-safety class. They also make sure that Chris buys a car that is highly rated for safety. As a final precaution, they restrict Chris from driving by herself until she is seventeen. Most important for financially defensive purposes, John and Sue add umbrella coverage to their insurance package.[7] While they have confidence in Chris and in the actions they have taken to make her a safe driver, they want to be sure that they are protected against claims due to death or injury.

Ken and Jennifer have reached retirement age. They have worked hard their entire lives and saved as much as they could. Now that retirement is near, they are excited—but also concerned. Their primary question is a simple one: Will their retirement savings outlast them?[8] Once they retire, they have no intention of returning to work. Although they have saved and invested on their own, they think it's time to get a second opinion.[9] So they meet with David, a certified financial planner who specializes in retirement-income analysis and can assess what they have and measure it against their likely use of funds. Using advanced retirement-planning software,[10] David reviews what Ken and Jennifer have and determines that they are properly funded and can retire if they wish. Because David knows that things can and do change, however, he advises Ken and Jennifer to review where they are annually, and even more often if major life changes occur.[11]

Albert is a first-rate estate attorney. He knows that his client, Ruth, has had problems with her daughter, Linda. Unfortunately, Linda has become addicted to drugs and has exhibited erratic and potentially dangerous behavior. Until now, Ruth has named Linda as her executor and successor trustee, but Albert is concerned that Linda's behavior makes her unsuitable for these important jobs. Albert explains his concerns to Ruth and convinces her that her son, Peter, would be a better choice for these roles. Although it pains Ruth to make these changes, she knows that Albert's advice is in her best interest and will actually help the entire family. In addition to the role change, Albert suggests that Ruth consider changing her trust to require Linda to be clean and sober for two years before receiving her inheritance. While Ruth thinks that this is a good idea, she is not yet emotionally ready to do this. Albert accepts her decision but advises Ruth that they should revisit this idea within the year. Ruth agrees.[12]

In each of these examples, defense has taken on an important role. In the game of Wealth Transfer and Distribution, we sometimes have to sit back and make sure that we have covered all the bases. When we review and reconsider, we often see that there are little things that we could do better. Planned review is one of the ways we make sure that what we intend to happen will actually happen.[13]

The Concept of Defense

Almost any game has concepts of offense and defense. In this chapter I focus on how the concept of defense affects our game. While defense in its simplest form is protection, defense can also become a form of offense when properly used. To paraphrase and invert one of the best-known axioms in sports, *the best offense is a good defense*. Without a good defense, the player is forced to rely solely on his ability to score points. A good defensive player, on the other hand, needs to score fewer points to win because he has limited his opponent's opportunities.[14]

When Chris Evert dominated tennis in the 1970s and '80s, she employed a strategy of wearing her opponent down by playing good defense. She became a "human backboard" who returned almost every shot played against her. Her extraordinary ability to respond forced her opponents into errors due to physical or mental fatigue—and those errors presented her with opportunities to score. While Chris's offense was certainly competent, her defense was the best.

The same approach can be taken in the game of Wealth Transfer and Distribution. By placing ourselves in strong defensive positions, we can employ a defensive strategy that wears our opponents down and effectively turns their fatigue into points for us. This may be a surprising notion to most people, given the popular view of the IRS as a giant, indefatigable monster. But the IRS, contrary to that impression, is just like any other corporation or entity; it has a limited amount of resources.

If you walk into a meeting with the IRS after it's threatened to audit you, and you're carrying a binder full of documents supporting your position, the conversation can change very quickly: The IRS may shift from an attack mode to a defensive posture. The agents may be knocked back on their heels because you've walked in there fully prepared to defend yourself,[15] and the IRS is unaccustomed to people defending themselves. If the likely cost of pursuing any given case exceeds the amount they might expect to recover, the IRS may well compromise. Tax authorities look for people who can't support their claims.[16] For the IRS, that's low-hanging fruit. They can make money on people who lie on their tax returns, but if you can defend yourself, you can beat the IRS.[17]

Make no mistake; defense is hard, dirty work that most players would prefer to avoid. However, well-played defense when transferring and distributing wealth can make a daunting situation more winnable.

The Game Is Rigged—or Is It?

Wealth Transfer and Distribution requires considerable attention to defensive strategy and tactics. Part of this is attributable to how the game is designed; most players feel uneasy when dealing with the IRS or other regulatory authorities. This apprehension is due in part to the belief that the IRS and the Tax Code are inherently unfavorable to the player because the rules and regulations limit what we can do. For this reason, it makes sense to spend some time discussing the unique and often misunderstood relationship between the player and his most dreaded opponent, the IRS.

There is some validity to the belief that the IRS is the player's worst nightmare. Prior to 1998, the burden of proof in tax matters rested with the taxpayer, rather than on the IRS or local tax authority. With a 1998 change to the Tax Code, however, the burden of proof shifted somewhat to the government.[18] There were strings attached to this change, however: The burden shifted " . . . only if the taxpayer introduces credible evidence relevant to determining his or her tax liability, cooperates with reasonable IRS requests, and complies with the recordkeeping and substantiation requirement in the code and regulations."[19] In other words, failure to meet these new standards shifted the burden of proof back to the player.

Even today, almost twenty years after this legislative change, many people continue to believe that tax law, unlike criminal law, assumes the taxpayer's guilt, and that the player must "prove his case"; even national legislators are guilty of this misunderstanding. As recently as 2013, Congressman Randy Forbes of Georgia said, "The IRS doesn't have to prove something against you. They can walk in and you've got the burden of proof."[20] The question then is how a player and his team can overcome a presumption so deeply rooted in the American psyche.

Answering this question returns us to the basics. One of the keys to successful wealth transfer and distribution is understanding the difference between fact and perception. The *fact* is that the onus of proof in tax matters is on the IRS, but many people believe the opposite, in part because of the intimidating resources the IRS has at its disposal and in part due to the prevalence of the myth.[21]

To counter this fear, the player needs to understand that the playing field is actually tilted in his favor if he marshals his data and builds his argument. While it is true that the IRS can use either of two approaches to attack the player—*form over substance* or *substance over form* (as we learned in chapter 3)—the player has an equal right to the same two arguments.

This means that special care must be given to understanding how to play defense against an opponent like the IRS. What makes the game harder to play is that these approaches can be used on a case-by-case basis, which means that there can be little continuity from case to case. Since this is a changing playing field, the player must identify which approach is being used and respond accordingly.[22] When confronted with a case of form over substance, she needs to understand that she benefits from going by the book, and basing her argument on a strict reading of the rules and regulations. When you take this position, there is black-and-white clarity; your position is either right or wrong. It's like using instant replay to make your case; when the player steps out bounds, the play ends. By contrast, substance over form takes the opposite position—that despite what the rules say, the player somehow broke with the *intention* of the game, and thus was in the wrong.

Because the IRS may argue either way on any case, the player is at a disadvantage unless he makes his case in the way that best presents his argument. This is why playing defense is so important, and one of the primary reasons why the pool of successful do-it-yourself players is so small; devising two forms of defense is difficult. Many players don't understand the importance of being prepared to meet the challenge of either interpretation of the rules.

At the end of the day, the player needs to believe that any dispute with tax authorities doesn't lead automatically to defeat. He needs to accept that he enjoys an important advantage when he follows the rules—namely, the presumption of innocence. While your opponents aren't obliged to help you build your case, you stand an excellent chance of winning if you play the game as it is meant to be played.

So, is the game rigged, at least as pertains to tax issues? Only if we allow it to be. Changing perception from weakness to strength is essential. Understanding that "good facts" can trump "bad facts" and "bad law" is equally important. Remember, no one is obliged to tell you how strong you are; *you* are obliged to determine your own strength and to use it to further your interests.

Using a Specialist to Find the White Lines

After all these factors have been taken into consideration, what happens when the game is actually played? This is where defense comes to life. Each game we play has different circumstances that require the player to determine how far she wishes to push the limits. For example, most players are familiar with the expression *crossing the white lines*. Just as lines are placed on our roadways to mark lanes whose confines must be respected, most sports use white lines to mark boundaries that players must observe— baselines, sidelines, etc. In our game, the concept of white lines takes on greater importance because the white lines can define both in-bounds and out-of-bounds, depending on which game we are playing.[23]

For example, in both basketball and football, any player touching the line is out of bounds, whereas in baseball the white lines bound the field. In our game, however, the IRS can use the white lines as it sees fit, and unless the player understands which interpretation of the white lines is being applied, he is at risk. Thus, not only is the form of argument critical, but so is a clear understanding of how far we can push the field of play before we approach or cross the line. Many of the most important games played in the history of Wealth Transfer and Distribution have hung on which interpretation of the lines was correct and whether the lines were crossed (recall our discussion in chapter 3 of the subjectivity of the strike zone in baseball).[24] In many of these cases, unintentionally crossing the lines doomed otherwise well-conceived defensive strategies.

As previously discussed in chapters 3 and 4, understanding the lines can therefore make all the difference in the world. Since our games are not always the same, this is an area in which team specialists earn their money and prove their value by devising the right defensive strategies and tactics to protect the player against the opponent's most likely attacks. While offensive shoot-outs in sports are spectacular to watch, they exhaust both offensive and defensive players. An impenetrable defense, while less entertaining, is a much more elegant and less exhausting way to win games. For this reason, the specialist who can build the successful defense is worth her weight.[25]

Second-Stringers and Relief Pitchers

Beyond these considerations, there are other aspects to building the right defense. For example, as a team owner, you need to have cash reserves to get the right players to fill out the roster. As managers, we want a good starting lineup appropriate to our game and its field of play, but we also need quality reserve players who can step in when needed. A great case in point recently was the second team for the NBA's 2015–2016 Golden State Warriors; when this group took the floor, they often got the same winning results as the first-stringers (as of this writing, the 2016-2017 second team performed equally as well)). In baseball, a starting pitcher will rarely stay in the game past the seventh inning. To pitch a full nine-inning game would be to risk giving up runs due to fatigue, or possibly even a debilitating shoulder injury. Consider Delores and Hal from the prologue: Delores, the independent widow, is the player, owner, and general manager, and Hal is her relief pitcher. He comes in and substitutes his authority for hers if and when a certain event occurs—that is, when Delores is no longer able to "pitch" for herself.

The concept of second-stringers or support players in our game is also applicable to trusts. In a trust, there is an original trustee, but there are also successor trustees. If, for whatever reason, the original trustee either can't or doesn't want to manage the trust anymore, the trust is still in play. It hasn't been distributed; we have a successor trustee.

Finally, relief pitchers are also needed in family-owned businesses. In a large enough family business, the owner is supported by a vice president, or by a CFO or financial officer of some kind (in a smaller company, that person might be just a bookkeeper). If something happens to the owner/president/ CEO, there is a succession plan in place; someone (often a family member) is available immediately to replace that leader and ensure a smooth transition to new management.[26]

How Long Do We Want to Depend on Our Defense?

Few teams can win the game by defense alone. Sooner or later, the offense must enter the game and contribute. While we want to make our point and defend our position, it should be with the intent of doing something with the results—like reaching our goal. Unless our goal is exclusively to defend a position, once we marshal our arguments and prove our point, it's time to move on. Defense may establish the base for our game plan, but sooner or later, it needs to yield the playing field to the offense.

The good news is that playing defense generally takes less energy than playing offense.[27] For this reason, while a strong defense is necessary, it also has its limits. Every team needs a clear understanding of the approach its defense will take and who the right specialists are to build and implement the right defense for each game. While we don't need a hammer to kill an ant, we will need a hammer to drive a nail. For these reasons, to develop the right defense game by game, a winning team needs financial capacity, team depth, and a sense of conservation to reach its potential. We'll discuss all three of these needs in the next section.[28]

The Importance of Bench Strength

Getting away from the game aspect for a moment, let's explore each of the above-mentioned additional requirements, starting with financial capacity and team depth. Having cash resources is critical in life as well as in any game. If the player wants to transfer a high-cash-flowing asset to his children (for example, a business, a dividend-paying stock, a piece of rental property—any kind of investment), he may well need alternative sources of cash to make up for the loss of cash flow if the transfer is to be completed while the player is still alive. In some cases, it is possible to make noncash flowing assets more fruitful, but whenever the owner/player decides to relinquish a source of cash flow, some consideration should be given to the need for alternative sources.

Similarly, the owner/player needs a strong capital-preservation strategy—that is, a strategy to maintain reserves in case something goes wrong. This is similar to having bench strength in any game. Without solid reserves, if something happens to a key player—for example, if he is injured or traded—the team and its strategy can be put at risk. Likewise, in the Wealth Transfer and Distribution game, a team's strategy can be put at risk if the owner lets his emotions overtake his good judgment and succumbs to the temptation to bet everything he has on an investment that later goes sour. Happily, most team owners/players are not inclined to put all their trust in single, high-risk opportunities. However, I have seen players put their health and well-being at risk by taking positions far too aggressive for their capacity to absorb loss.

Owners need to be able to substitute players when circumstances make such action necessary. For example, while the owner's heir apparent may be his first son, an accident may befall that son, resulting in his disability or even death. Or in a less dramatic scenario, the owner or the designated heir may simply change his mind. Either circumstance brings about the need for a ready backup. With these possibilities in mind, having multiple skilled players at each position never hurt any team. While these bench players may not initially be as strong as the starting players, with time and experience, they'll have the potential to develop into strong players in their own right.[29]

"Know When to Fold 'Em"

Finally, conservation helps everyone. It makes no sense to fight a lost battle, and there is no shame in acknowledging defeat; we are not meant to win every game. Sometimes it makes sense to call it a day and learn from our defeats. There are times when owner/players take on battles they can't win. While a loss may be disappointing, it may also hold the key to ultimate success. I have seen a few clients continue to pursue unwinnable goals, even ignoring the counsel of specialists tasked with helping them develop winning defenses. Some games can't be won, and it is better to acknowledge when this is the case. By doing so, we can turn our attention to situations that offer more favorable prospects. In any case, making sure you don't exhaust your defense resources is critical.

———————•◆•———————

The combination of good strategic defense with healthy tactical reserves enables the manager and the player to expend as little energy as possible on a successful defensive scheme, leaving an excess of capacity for offense. By keeping the defense rested and prepared, the team is poised to protect its advantage and score more points. Good defense makes playing offense easier.

When we play defense in the Wealth Transfer and Distribution game, we want to think and act like the three hundred Spartans at Thermopylae, who held off the greatest army in the world and gave the rest of Greece the breather it needed. An effective defense can keep your team in the game, and in many cases, position your team to *win* the game. In more cases, however, an effective defense will enable your offense to pressure your opponents into making mistakes (as Chris Evert did to her opponents), and this strategy will deliver ultimate victory. In our game, a great defense that understands its opponent and the field of play can lay the groundwork for victory. Defense isn't pretty, and oftentimes it is hard, dirty work. But it is the necessary foundation of your team's success.

Notes

1. For guidance on charitable deductions, see "Substantiating Charitable Contributions," *IRS. gov*.
2. Section 529 plans are tax-advantaged savings plans to pay for college education. For a good overview of 529 plans, see "An Introduction to 529 Plans," US Securities and Exchange Commission website. One of the benefits of 529 plans is that they allow front-loading, the ability to make multiyear gifts in a single year. For example, with a five-year limit, you can gift $70,000 to a 529 account in one year. As pointed out in the text, however, making more than one year's gift imposes a time-out on other gifts to the same person (please note: in this case, a year refers to a tax year and not a calendar year; for example, by making a two-year gift on December 31, 2015, Eric can make gifts again as early as January 1, 2017).
3. "Powers of Attorney Come in Different Flavors," *Elder Law Answers*, March 4, 2015. For information on financial powers, see "Financial Power of Attorney," AARP website. For information on medical powers, see "Giving Someone a Power of Attorney for Your Health Care," *The Commission on Law and Aging, American Bar Association,* 2011.
4. "Five Things to Know About Safe Deposit Boxes, Home Safes, and Your Valuables," *FDIC*, Fall 2009.
5. Many advisors shy away from assisting clients in fiduciary matters. Investment professionals often are forbidden to assist by their broker-dealers. Attorneys or accountants can be limited by their liability carriers. However, I expect that this practice may change in the future. In my case, I surrendered my securities licenses and became a professional fiduciary specifically to assist clients who had no other options. For reassurance that fiduciary services are needed, and that providing them is worthwhile, see Alexander A. Bove Jr., "Conquering the Fear of Fiduciary Duty," *Trusts & Estates*, May 2016, pages 60–62. Obviously, anyone taking the fiduciary step needs to be aware of recent developments; see Carly E. Howard and Michael Sneeringer, "Fiduciary Law Trends," *Trusts & Estates,* May 2016, pages 56–59.
6. Giving authority to others is often overlooked in planning. For an introduction to advance directives, see Jamie Zuckerman, "Why Do So Few Americans Have Advance Directives," *WealthManagement.com*, April 18, 2016. At the same time, giving authority to others, especially medical authority, requires special care. Consider the case of terminal illness; see Tisa Pedersen, "California's End of Life Option Act," *Steve Leimberg's Estate Planning Newsletter*, August 4, 2016. Also see Michael Brevda, "Seven Signs of Potential Elder Abuse," *WealthManagement.com*, July 20, 2016.
7. "About Umbrella Coverage," *GEICO*. Umbrella coverage is used to protect family assets from liabilities attributable to young drivers.

8. Kevin McKinley, "Protecting Pension Recipients," *Wealth Management.com*, July 18, 2016. Also see "Advisors Underestimate Clients' Concerns About Health Care Costs and Taxes," *Advisor News*, June 13, 2016. Also see Chuck Carnevale, "Answers to the Hardest Decision—When Do I Sell a Stock?" *Advisor Perspectives*, June 23, 2016; David J. Yvars Sr., "Combining a CRT with Long-term Insurance," *Trusts & Estates*, June 21, 2016; and Carol Einhorn and Steve Leimberg, "What Every Professional Should Know About LTCI in 2015," *Steve Leimberg's Elder Care Law Planning Newsletter*, March 11, 2015.

9. Amy Florian, "Are You Ready for the Coming Death Boom?" *WealthManagement.com*, July 5, 2016. This article briefly discusses the "soft" benefits (like grief counseling) provided by financial advisors. While the emphasis is still most often on answering financial questions, we see more and more examples of the need for personal services in financial-advisory relationships.

10. For examples of software that companies use to identify potential investment risk, see Ryan W. Neal, "LPL Turns to HiddenLevers' Technology for DOL Compliance," *Intelligent Advisor*, September 9, 2016 or "UBS Wants to Use AI to Help Clients Invest Their Money," *Reuters*, September 13, 2016. Another tool is described here: Chris Taylor, "Your Money: Can Comic Books Teach Kids Money Smarts?" *Money*, May 12, 2016. This article highlights a comic book designed to educate children about money and refers to Genworth's R70i Aging Experience, which illustrates the limitations of aging and deterioration.

11. Simple changes in our investing environment can upset planning, for example, when perceived guarantees disappear. See Daisy Maxey, "Five Things Investors Should Know about New Rules on Money-Market Funds," *The Wall Street Journal*, August 9, 2016.

12. For an overview on the benefits of trust (and planning) reviews, see Steve Parrish, "Trust Me, You Should Review Your Trusts," *Forbes*, December 14, 2015. For a compelling and more formal argument for the benefits of planned reviews, see Steve Oshins and Boo Keebler, "U.S. v. Kimball, Jr. and the U.S.'s Attempt to Attach a Tax Lien to a Gift Trust," *Steve Leimberg's Asset Protection Planning Newsletter*, July 19, 2016.

13. "Executor & Trustee Guidelines," *Fidelity*. Also see John Palley, "Ten Characteristics of a Good Trustee," *California Probate Attorney*, March 17, 2014.

14. Defensive behavior is oftentimes fear based. We feel at risk and we assume a defensive position. For an excellent article on the role of fear in our game, see Matt Oechsli, "Your Clients' Greatest Motivator," *WealthManagement.com*, May 19, 2016. Another approach to fear is to secure peace of mind; see "How Advisors Can Benefit from Spotting Out-of-Date Estate Plans," *WealthManagement.com*, May 18, 2016.

15. Sometimes it is possible to secure victories over the IRS even when facts and circumstances are *not* in our favor; see Keith Schiller, *Estate Planning at the Movies*®, (Bloomberg BNA, 2014), and "PLR 201548004 Brings Belated Happiness with a Late Portability Election in the Spirit of the Breakfast Club," *Steve Leimberg's Estate Planning Newsletter*, January 14, 2016.

16. For a case in which "bad facts" led to a bad outcome, see Owen Fiore, "Estate of Sarah D. Holliday v. Commissioner: Another in a Long Line of Tax Cases Considering Application of IRC Section 2036(a)," *Steve's Leimberg's Estate Planning Newsletter*, March 28, 2016. For a great outcome, see Steve Leimberg, "Purdue: Gifts of LLC Interest Excludable, Qualify for Annual Exclusion, and Interest on Loans from Beneficiaries Deductible," *Steve Leimberg's Estate Planning Newsletter*, January 11, 2016. The outcome in the second case was a clear example of "good" facts, good argument, good business purpose, and a good outcome!

17. For a common man's victory, see Peter. J. Reilly, "Grandfather Beats IRS in Tax Court without Lawyer," *Forbes*, September 15, 2014. While we commonly think of the tax authorities as our opponents, it is important to remember that family members can be equally challenging. To learn how to insulate against family contests, see Barbara R.

Grayson, "Minimize Litigation Risks in Estate Plans," *Trusts & Estates,* May 2016, pages 43–46.

18. George S. Jackson, "The Burden of Proof in Tax Controversies," *The CPA Journal,* 1999.

19. https://www.treasury.gov/tigta/iereports/2010reports/2010IER002fr.html; also see Ray A. Knight and Lee G. Knight, "Shifting the Burden of Proof," *Journal of Accountancy,* August 31, 1999.

20. Neil H. Buchanan, "Bad Journalism, Again: Fact Checkers Think That Facts Are a Matter of Opinion," *Dorf on Law,* June 13, 2013.

21. Despite appearances to the contrary, you *can* fight city hall. TD Ameritrade has created an avenue for registered investment advisors (RIAs) to make their voices heard in Washington; see "Listen Up! TD Ameritrade Institutional's New Advocacy Tool Gives Voice to RIAs," *Business Wire,* October 6, 2015.

22. John Mauldin, "Negative Rates Nail Savers," *Thoughts From the Frontline,* September 14, 2016.

23. Asset classes can serve defensive purposes; see Jared Dillian, "Title Here," *The 10th Man,* September 15, 2016.

24. In almost any year there are significant court decisions, many of which favor the taxpayer. For an overview of 2015, see Steve R. Akers, "Heckerling Musings 2016 and Current Developments," *Bessemer Trust,* February 2016. This outstanding compendium provides overviews and insights into cases where taxpayers prevailed or lost. For court cases that benefitted the taxpayer, see *"Estate of Purdue v. Commissioner,"* pages 54–60; *"Estate of William Davidson,"* pages 64–68; "Rejuvenating Stale Irrevocable Trusts Through Trust-to-Trust Transfers," pages 79–93; *"Estate of Edward Redstone v. Commissioner,'* pages 113–119; *"Green v. United States,"* page 122; and "Do Not Concede That Annual Exclusion Is Lost if Crummey Notices Not Given Timely," pages 137–138. Each of these summaries proves the point that our player, the taxpayer, can win—and win big—if he or she puts in the necessary time and effort. In any given year it is possible to find significant taxpayer victories. Equally important but less advertised, however, are the little victories that get no attention, and those victories, big and small, that are achieved without court direction.

25. For a helpful article on bench strength, see Guido M.J. de Koning, "Building Your 'Bench Strength,'" *Gallup,* March 10, 2005.

26. For an overview to both internal and external threats, see Anna Sulkin, "Family Businesses Fear External Factors as Greatest Threat to Success," *Trusts & Estates,* September 14, 2016.

27. Dr. George Simon, "An Offense Is Not a Defense," *Counselling Resource,* October 23, 2008. While this article pertains to behavior, its opening statement captures the essence of offense and defense: "An offense involves fighting hard enough to secure a goal and remove obstacles to that goal. A defense involves expending just enough energy to ward off an attack or prevent injury."

28. For a quick example of how all these factors come together, see Dennis Webb, "Audit-Proofing Checklist for Recent Gifts of Interest in Real Estate," *Steve Leimberg's Estate Planning Newsletter,* September 11, 2014.

29. Todd Fithian, Albert E. Gibbons, and David W. Holaday, "High Performance Teaming and Professional Collaboration," *Trusts & Estates,* May 2016, page 22.

Chapter 8

Playing Offense

———————◆———————

Prologue

n the last chapter I stated that defense is hard, dirty work. By contrast, playing offense is fun and potentially exciting. In fact, for most players, nothing in the game of Wealth Transfer and Distribution is more appealing than playing offense. It's actually getting to the plate and getting the chance to hit the ball. Defense is creating a baseline, setting the table, and being sure that you've got your ducks in a row. Once you have those ducks in a row, however, you'll want to exercise your power and move forward. That's offense.

Offense requires a different kind of creativity than playing defense; when we play offense, we seek out goals or objectives that satisfy wants instead of needs. Meeting needs with defensive or baseline tactics gives us a sense of safety; it makes us feel protected. Once our needs are met, we can turn our attention to the fulfillment of other desires.

Focusing on wants changes our point of view; we direct our attention to objectives that deliver tangible results like increased wealth, revenues, or profits. Addressing what we *need*—a defensive action—gives us a sense of protection and safety; addressing what we *want*, by comparison, elevates us and helps us grow. I think a review of three successful offensive outcomes might help to illustrate what successful offensive play looks like.

Cindy is one of my favorite clients. When we started working together she had recently been widowed.[1] While she had significant assets, she had relied on her husband's guidance through the years when making her financial decisions. When he died, she was unsure what to do. Now, for the first time ever, she was obliged to take charge of her life.

When we first began our relationship, despite her high net worth, Cindy's first question at every meeting was invariably, "Am I okay?" I get asked this question a lot, actually, and the anxiety—the raw *fear*—that prompts a client to ask it can sometimes be paralyzing for them.[2]

After several years of patient effort, she came to understand that she didn't need high returns to enjoy her life and her wealth. What she needed was consistent performance and controlled risk.[3] Once these two needs were met, she was able to turn her attention to playing offense. She learned that her spending was never going to be an issue because she was conservative by nature, and that by establishing clear goals and objectives and managing to them, success could come easily to her. Now, more than ten years after her husband's death, Cindy manages her wealth comfortably, with a high degree of confidence that her money will outlive her and benefit those close to her. Cindy's ensuing offensive gains made it possible for her to reward herself with trips to Europe, changes to her house, and gifts to family members.

Cindy's life changed dramatically once she decided to take an investment account that had grown significantly and turn it into an additional source of cash flow by repositioning it in order to sell it. To accomplish this, she married the twin goals of providing for herself and benefitting charity; she established a charitable trust.[4] She then repositioned the investment account, placing it within the trust, and sold it from there.

A charitable trust is a planning opportunity that exists within the Tax Code, and it allows us to do a number of important and useful things: We get to sell something without creating an immediate taxable event. We also get to take an asset that was appreciating but delivering little cash flow and alter its nature so that its primary benefit becomes higher than market-rate income. This is done by either transforming it into an annuity with a fixed-dollar annual payout or changing it to a fixed-percentage annual payout—either of which can be accomplished by placing it within the charitable trust. Finally, we set aside an interest for charity, which in this case, transfers when Cindy dies. Simply put, creating a charitable trust allowed Cindy to defer taxes on the sale of her asset, generate a high-dollar lifetime cash stream, and deliver benefit to charities when she passed.[5] The extra funds from this redeployment of assets allowed her to expand her lifestyle and to move beyond her husband's death.

Terry and Jo faced a different set of obstacles to playing offense the way they wanted to. In their case, the obstacle was their three children, who needed to learn how to be financially responsible. When younger generations begin to understand the real benefits of wealth, playing offense can be great fun.[6] Unfortunately, Terry and Jo's children had not learned some basic life lessons, especially concerning money. Oftentimes one of the biggest hurdles affluent families face is children who think that money grows on trees. Terry and Jo needed to get their children financially grounded. To do this, we decided to set up a little business and to encourage the children to take active roles in it.

Terry and Jo gifted starter funds to the children, but left them to decide for themselves what type of business they would run. Once this was determined, Terry and Jo worked with the children on everything from budgeting to production. However, they limited their assistance to words of wisdom and guidance; they allowed the kids to err, and to suffer the consequences of their mistakes. Within a fairly short time, the business began to perform surprisingly well. The children, far from being reluctant participants, actually wanted to put their own money at risk. They became true owners. This was a terrific example of offense being played at the highest level: Terry and Jo had a *want*—to teach their children to appreciate the value of money and the importance of hard work and wise decision-making—and the steps they took to ensure that the children learned these lessons were the *epitome* of good offensive play.[7]

Not all efforts at offense succeed or come from where you would expect. In many ways, Henry and Lucille were models of financial success who seized every opportunity to help their children. When it came to planning for the transfer of their wealth upon their deaths, however, Henry and Lucille hid their heads. Although they had always said that it was important to prepare for the costs associated with death, Henry and his wife took no action. Henry was so concerned about his enjoyment of the present moment that he ignored the inevitable.

Happily, Henry and Lucille's children, Mark and Jill, had learned their financial lessons well. Seeing that their parents' inaction was threatening to burden them with the high costs of settling the estate, Mark and Jill decided to use their own funds to offset those costs. To prepare themselves for the major tax event they knew would accompany their parents' deaths, they used some of their own funds to protect the estate. They asked their parents to submit to life insurance exams, and by allocating a relatively small amount of money annually, the children created the reserve necessary to offset the cost of transferring the estate from their parents to themselves.[8] Getting all parties to agree wasn't the easiest thing in the world, but the result was one of the best family decisions that could have been made. Rather than having to pay several million dollars to the IRS, Mark and Jill made a sacrifice to ensure that their parents' hard work and success would be delivered downstream.[9]

———— ♦ ————

Sometimes the greatest gratification comes from learning that you are capable of making good financial decisions. In other cases, a player may derive satisfaction from the knowledge that family members or charities will benefit from her lifetime of hard work and careful planning. What makes offense fun is the sense of accomplishment one feels when it has been done well. Unlike other approaches in this book, success from a good offensive effort can be measured by the smallest accomplishment or the most sophisticated set of changes. In the end, the thrill of devising a good offense and the satisfaction of success are what keep us engaged with the game of Wealth Transfer and Distribution.[10]

The Makings of a Good Offense

This chapter on playing offense is a complement to our discussion of defense. Combining good offense with good defense puts any player in a position to compete, and that is what drives the game of Wealth Transfer and Distribution. Once the defense is set and proven ready, the owner, manager, coaches, and player can turn their collective attention to scoring points.

A few caveats are in order, however: Since we emphasized the importance of conservation in the discussion on defense, some players may feel inclined to be aggressive when playing offense. Some players feel that money saved by crafting a good defense should now be used to fund a good offense. In fact, there is no good argument for this tactic. Conservation, whether of talent, energy, money, or time, makes as much sense on offense as it did on defense. In fact, successful players take the same conservative approach to playing offense that they did to playing defense.

Conservation and conservatism shouldn't be equated with a lack of imagination or courage. Rather, to be conservative on offense means to fight the battles that can be won, spend as little as necessary for success, take advantage of your opponent's weaknesses, and use the rules to your advantage. The purpose of a successful offense is not to slaughter your opponent; it is to win with the least amount of expended resources or effort. In playing offense, it is downright foolish to waste assets.[11]

This approach requires yet another exploration of goals and objectives. First and foremost, the purpose of playing offense is to win. Second, winning should be accomplished with economy and elegance. In chapter 6, we considered the concepts of effectiveness and efficiency; these are worth a second review here. Effectiveness is getting from where we are to where we want to be; efficiency is getting there with the fewest stops in between. The best offense, then, plays the game effectively (scoring points) with the fewest deviations (unnecessary or wasteful actions). When we have an effective and efficient offense, we can score points and win the game quickly and easily. This victory requires the best use of offensive assets. What are our offensive assets? They include (but are not limited to) time, appreciation, leverage, and compounding.

Time

In my opinion, time is the most valuable resource we have when playing offense. Effective use of time can both suffocate an opponent's opportunity to score and enhance *our* opportunity to do so. For example, recall our discussion in chapter 3 of the "four-corners offense"; North Carolina's Tar Heels would hold onto the ball, dribbling it until the clock ran out and preventing their opponents from scoring. In our game, it is the player himself who most often runs out the clock on his own offensive opportunities; we are all too frequently our own worst enemies. We all know people who spend inordinate and inexplicable amounts of time on trivial matters. In our game, this is one of the biggest and most wasteful errors.

Time is inventory, and every player has limited inventory. When playing the game, the player's team needs to value time. Assume for the moment that we want to argue a case in which the difference between winning and losing is x. Does this value merit the time spent? It might if x equals $1 million; it might not if x equals $1,000. Too many times I have seen people fail to weigh carefully the time needed to win against the value at stake.

Value is not always monetary, however. Sometimes value is tactical or strategic in nature. Let's assume that winning a point on a small matter opens the floodgates to a larger matter; is it worth the time to win this point? Certainly. Thus, when looking at the value of time for offense, a small victory today may create a larger opportunity tomorrow.

A good example of this would be the treatment of minority interests in closely held companies and real estate in estate planning. For the past twenty-five years, tax discounts for minority interest and lack of marketability have been the foundation for successful family transfers and distributions.[12] It has long been accepted that a minority shareholder does not have enough power or authority within an enterprise to stop the majority holder from taking action. At the same time, there may be shortage of outside buyers with an appetite for a small interest in a family-owned position. Thus, when this minority shareholder goes to sell her interest, she is often obliged to sell it at a discount that doesn't reflect her real percentage holding in the company's value—and that discount is reflected in the proportionately lower tax she pays on the money she earns from that sale. Unfortunately, families were for many years treated unfairly in this arena; if you wanted to sell stock to a family member at a price that reflected its lower value as a minority share, the IRS would consider it a gift . . . with concomitant tax consequences for the recipient.

The unfairness of this disparity eventually became so evident that in 1990, Congress acknowledged the financial consequences to families of discounting minority-interest value, and passed appropriate legislation to put families on a level playing field: the Revenue Reconciliation Act of 1990. With this legislation in hand, specialists began to look for expanded uses for it elsewhere, and today we have minority shareholders in companies worth billions arguing that their interests should be subject to discounts during their lifetimes as well as at death. This practice has given rise to highly specialized planning techniques focused on lowering the value of family interests in family-owned businesses for estate-planning purposes. As a result of this legislation and its consequences, the IRS collects only a fraction of the taxes it would have without this concession. Here is a clear case of time spent on a small matter—albeit in this case, time spent by Congress—leading to extraordinarily high benefits. It must also be noted that the effect of these acts has become a problem of such magnitude that the IRS and Treasury are currently exploring ways to eliminate what they perceive to be an easily abused loophole. If successful, this change would have adverse effects on family transfers and distributions and lead to significantly higher tax collections.[13]

There is another aspect to time as an offensive weapon: In some cases, players have limited windows of opportunity. Congress sometimes enacts laws known as *extenders* to provide certain taxpayers with advantages for narrowly specified periods of time. This is similar to-time added for stoppage in a soccer match. While each half is set at forty-five minutes, additional time is added for delay of game or injury. This extends the playing time and creates scoring opportunity for both teams. Thus, if a team is behind and the clock is ticking down to the end of the game, it may be advantageous for a player to fake an injury, thereby lengthening the game and providing his team with a little more time to score in a game that they would otherwise have lost. This deception (if it can be called that—in most cases, the other team, the officials, and the spectators all have a pretty good idea what's really going on) has the added benefit of allowing his teammates time to recover some of their energy before resuming the game. After a short recovery period, the "injured" player's team may be able to score a last-second point. Obviously, the opposing team also enjoys the same recovery time, but playing offense requires more energy than playing defense, so this respite is therefore more valuable to the "injured" player's offensive teammates than to the other team's defense.

In our game, a similar thing has happened in Congress in recent years. As Congress nears the end of its term, usually in mid-December, it passes laws retroactive to January 1 of the same year. Historically Congress has passed legislative extenders for periods as short a couple of weeks. For many years, the upshot of this practice has been that taxpayers had no way to know until the very end of the year whether Congress would allow them to make use of certain tax concessions. While taxpayers obviously can't go back in time, they can still act, even with a narrow window of opportunity.[14]

A case in point is a charitable gifting extender for taxpayers over 70½ years old who have large IRA accounts and strong philanthropic interests. This extender allows the player to make up to $100,000 in charitable gifts from an IRA account without recording the withdrawal or the gift on his tax return, so long as this action is completed no later than December 31. While the benefit of this action varies from player to player, in many cases not having to post this activity on his tax return can save the player money. Despite the fact that it may deliver only small tax savings, the very existence of this opportunity requires the attention of the player, the owner, and some specialists during one of the busiest times of the year. It is important to note, however, that improper or incorrect use of this concession can create more problems than it's worth. For example, failure to complete all the required steps prior to December 31 can trigger higher taxes.

That said, this extender was important enough that before Congress made it permanent in 2015, many players would wait until the last fifteen days of the calendar year to play this game. Interested individuals, along with their investment advisors and their legal counsel, would go so far as to draw up the anticipated paperwork earlier in the year so that when the window of opportunity opened, they could move on it quickly.

Another aspect of the time element of offensive planning is tempo. In recent years, college football teams have begun pressuring opposing defenses by accelerating the tempo of plays. Instead of shuffling players in and out of the lineup, many college teams—especially those that depend on speed in their offense—force the action by playing faster. These teams run several plays in a row with minimal time between plays. This change in tempo pressures the defense (which is prohibited from substituting fresh players by rule), and it can lead to quicker scores or defensive errors. The same approach is available to our player: Accelerated tempo can be used in the wealth-transfer process to push the IRS to a faster result than ordinarily expected.

An example of how this can occur might help. Under normal circumstances, when an estate tax filing is made, the IRS has three years to review the estate tax return before issuing a closing letter. However, the player can impose a quicker process on the IRS by asking them to accelerate the closing-letter date; this can shorten the IRS's review period to as little as nine months. Obviously, there is a substantial difference between thirty-six months and nine months when it comes to reviewing a complicated estate tax filing.[15]

Unfortunately, in many cases, this opportunity is lost or ignored because the player or members of his team are unaware of this option or choose not to exercise it. That's a shame, given the fact that high-value estates almost certainly will be audited. Isn't it better to impose a shorter audit time on the IRS (especially given that the IRS has fewer resources for review than in the past due to budgetary cutbacks)? And if the estate is well organized and has the team assembled to defend the return, doesn't it make sense to accelerate the process so that the facts at hand are as fresh as possible for everyone?

As with a hurry-up offense in football, the player can impose a timing requirement that can work to the player's advantage. This is especially true in those circumstances in which the estate can substantiate its positions. In this instance, the player pushing for faster response has also played good defense by making sure that the issues of form and substance have already been addressed. Being able to require the IRS to preform according to the player's timetable changes the tempo of the game.

Appreciation

Other important offensive weapons in the game of Wealth Transfer and Distribution are appreciation, leverage, and compounding. Appreciation combined with the use of time can make an offensive strategy work very effectively.[16] The player who can achieve incremental growth has the ability to play longer and, hopefully, more effectively. A good example of this is the checker player who gets kings. Kings, an appreciated asset in comparison to an ordinary checker, have the flexibility to move in every direction, which amplifies the player's ability to take advantage of opportunities across the board. At the same time, this ability to move in every direction carries with it a defensive benefit: the ability to avoid problems by moving backward to skirt trouble. Similarly, with our game, appreciation of assets allows the player to reduce risk at the same time that it allows him to compound value. This double-edged ability gives the player plenty of opportunity to play the game better, taking advantage of opportunity while sitting out bad times.

When we grow an investment, we create the opportunity for risk control and greater diversification. For example, if our investment appreciates from $5,000 to $10,000, we can return our initial position to its starting value and reallocate excess funds to a new holding. By doing this, we double our holdings. To put this in simpler terms, we hold onto the $5,000 we have made and reinvest only the original $5,000. Think of it in the same way you would think about playing blackjack in a casino: If we're wise, we come to the casino with only as much money as we feel comfortable losing—let's say, for example, $100. If we have a lucky streak, we pocket our winnings as we play and continue to place bets only with that initial $100; once that $100 is gone, it's time to go home . . . hopefully with a few hundred dollars more than we came in with. If we've had a bad night, however, we're only down by $100.

We should take a similar approach to investing, but—and here's where we must abandon the blackjack metaphor—we must also *diversify* as we play, investing in different places each time we return our money to the table. If our $5,000 asset appreciates to $10,000, we take the $5,000 we have earned and reinvest it elsewhere. If we were to do this several times, by the third or fourth iteration, we would have a portfolio of four to eight positions that, if well chosen, would both mitigate risk and expand our interests. This is the outcome of not having all your eggs in one basket. Using appreciation to our advantage changes how the game is played; instead of dependence on a single investment or asset, we have multiple assets or investments working for us and protecting our flanks.[17]

Leverage

Leverage is another significant offensive weapon. In wealth transfer and distribution, leverage is a tool reserved generally for players with larger bankbooks. In this case, larger bankbooks provide better borrowing credentials, which in turn enables the player to qualify more easily for the use of someone else's money, and to borrow greater amounts. Using someone else's money enables us to expand our ability to play without spreading ourselves too thin—and this is leverage.[18]

Effectively, this amounts to the rich getting richer. But the player who can use leverage needs to use it judiciously.[19] Leverage doesn't have the two-sided benefit of appreciation, with which additional gains allow the player to actually take funds off the playing field. Leverage requires the player to absorb additional risk—a capacity made possible by past success. *Over*-leveraging, however, strips our successful player of assets faster than if leveraging weren't used at all. Therefore the player should use leverage carefully, and have an exit plan in mind. When the player absorbs more risk in order to acquire more leverage, she should have a specific, well-defined time and dollar limit in mind. The best thing we can do with leverage is to use it as necessary and retire it sooner than demanded. When it comes to leverage, smaller, less powerful teams and players are often at a disadvantage compared to their more prosperous competitors.[20]

A good example of this occurs in baseball, where the small-market teams have to compete with larger and richer adversaries. The Oakland A's are a classic example of this. Compared to the Yankees or the Angels, the A's have little leverage. As a result, they are forced to think differently; rather than pursue established stars who demand more financial resources, the A's look to secure younger players who demand smaller contracts. At the same time, because they can't afford to over-leverage, they are forced to rid themselves of strong players before those players' contract demands get too high. As a result, unlike their large-market competitors, the A's remake their team almost every year, looking for bargains and operating within a smaller cost framework. Both the Yankees and the Angels, by virtue of their large-market advantages, can leverage themselves on players who demand long-term, high-dollar contracts year after year. Does this mean that the A's can't compete? The answer is clearly no, but in order to compete, they need to excel at identifying bargains and do an even better job of avoiding mistakes.

Leverage thus gives the large-market teams an advantage when it is used properly. So long as these teams are more right than wrong, they can gamble with leverage because their capacity to accept risk is so much higher. Having access to less leverage is not the end of the world, however. It is still possible to compete with less capacity; it simply requires more careful consideration and better planning. Irrespective of size, leverage is something worth having available even if it isn't always used.

Compounding

Compounding is our last offensive consideration. For many players, compounding is a confusing idea. Compounding is more than appreciation; it is effectively growth on our principal *and* on that principal's growth. For example, assume I promise you individual payments of 6 percent on $1,000 every year for twelve years; this means that I add $60 to your account every anniversary. On the other hand, let's assume that I offer you 6 percent *compounded* for twelve years. At the end of twelve years, using a compounded approach, I would give you more than $2,000! The difference between collecting $60 per year plus our original $1,000 back (which adds up to $1,720 over twelve years) and collecting a total of $2,000 is the effect of compounding. And over longer periods, the effect of compounding becomes much more dramatic; over the course of thirty years, that initial $1,000 turns into $5,743! This appreciation can occur over the course of your entire working life, between the age at which you first begin to make disposable income and the day you finally retire. Many people have called compounding "the eighth wonder of the world," and rightly so.[21]

Any time the player can accumulate more resources and capacity by maintaining the current course of action, he will be better off. Consider gardening (while not a sport *per se*, gardening can become very competitive in certain neighborhoods, and it will be a useful metaphor for this discussion). If the first player can plant his garden perfectly the first time, he maximizes the benefit of compounding. By doing everything right the first time, his job is subsequently limited to maintenance: pruning, weeding, and tending. The reason for this simple: Everything he has planted grows successfully and flourishes. By contrast, his neighbor may have picked the wrong plants; he may have under-watered, he may have overwatered, he may have not used the right fertilizer, or he may have used too much fertilizer. Because of these miscalculations, he is forced to plant and replant, expending time, effort, and money while our gardener simply tends to what he has, trimming as required and maintaining as needed. Successful compounding minimizes the expenditure of energy; the player who benefits from compounding is not spending time or money determining what didn't work and attempting to correct it. He is content with letting his garden grow.[22]

In sports, this is similar to having a good minor-league system. By assembling a network of capable scouts who identify the best prospects and minor-league managers who successfully develop these prospects, and by choosing wisely which prospects to keep and which to bundle for trades, even a weaker team can compete strongly with teams that don't get this right.

In investing, for example, whether we discuss stocks or real estate, the best results theoretically would come from the portfolio whose assets never need to be sold. Sam Zell, a world-famous real estate mogul, allegedly is proud to have a property in Michigan that he purchased when he was in college. That property today generates more in annual cash flow than its original cost. In effect, this is close to the perfect investment. In our game of Wealth Transfer and Distribution, success in compounding can spell the difference between a team that reloads and a team that rebuilds. Rebuilding is much more expensive, in terms of both money and time. The ability to do things right the first time makes it possible for the team with fewer initial resources to outbid and outmaneuver the team that needs to start all over again, even if that team has more initial resources.

Obviously, even with the strongest offensive strategies and tactics, it is possible for a team to lose. Playing good offense is not a guarantee of victory . . . but it does position a team more favorably to win. A team that has a nearly impregnable defense but scores no points will not win; it is the combination of good defense with good offense that allows a well-managed team to dominate. Having any of these characteristics makes a team better, but the best teams have it all: good management, sound philosophy, strong defense, and electric offense. However, we also need to consider carefully *when* we choose to play the game. That leads us to our next consideration: the season's schedule.

Notes

1. Life is difficult enough when a spouse dies, but what happens when the deceased spouse is an expatriate? See Chuck Rubin, "Marital Deduction Trusts and Covered Expatriates—More Questions than Answers," *Steve Leimberg's International Tax Planning Newsletter,* May 17, 2016. Tax matters are also challenging for surviving spouses who live in Common Law states; for a way to enjoy the same basis step-up at the death of a spouse as citizens in Community Property states, see Austin Bramwell, Brad Dillon, and Leah Socash, "Step-Up Personal Residence Trusts (SUPRTs) and Other Grantor-Retained Interest Step-Up Trusts (GRISUTs)," *Steve Leimberg's Estate Planning Newsletter,* November 30, 2015. Also see James M. Kane, "Income Tax Planning Using the Delaware Tax Trap," *Steve Leimberg's Estate Planning Newsletter*, March 30, 2015, and Michael S. Fischer, "Easing the Real Estate Tax Hit," *Private Wealth*, October 30, 2014.

2. For further reading on this phenomenon, see Christopher Robbins, "Are Clients in Denial About Retirement Readiness?" *Financial Advisor,* September 28, 2016.

3. For an example of consistent performance and controlled risk, and to understand how savings for college costs can handle both sides of this economic equation; see Michael Kitces, "Liquidate Appreciated Securities Tax-Free for College Funding by Avoiding the Kiddie-Tax," *Advisor Perspectives,* September 26, 2016. Also see Blanche Lark Christerson, "Tax Topics 2016–06," *Deutsche Bank Wealth Management,* June 24, 2016.

4. For examples of how the two varieties of charitable remainder trusts work, see "Charitable Trusts Help You Reach Many Goals," *AboutGiving.net,* October 2016. For a very basic overview of charitable lead and remainder trusts, see "Basics of Charitable Trusts," *Wilmington Trust.* This area of planning can be extremely complicated and requires outside help and counsel. For this reason, the references here are decidedly basic. At the same time, understanding how to transition from appreciation to total return (an often-used

in conjunction with charitable trusts) is essential. For information on this issue, see Chuck Carnevale, "Dividends' True Contribution to Total Return May Surprise You," *Advisor Perspectives,* March 3, 2016; also see Chuck Carnevale, "Which Is Best—Investing for Income or Total Return," *Advisor Perspectives,* March 14, 2016.

5. For a superb, detailed overview on strategies and tactics in charitable giving, see *Trusts & Estates,* October 2015. This entire edition is dedicated to current thinking on giving. For a new twist on giving, see Richard Fox, "Is Mark Zuckerberg's Limited Liability Company the New Model for Charitable Giving?" *Steve Leimberg's Charitable Planning Newsletter,* March 22, 2016.

6. For more on this topic, see Deborah Erdmann and Nicole Shrive, "'How to Prepare Children for Wealth," *Premier Trust,* 2014, Michael M. Pompian, "Intergenerational Wealth Transfer," *Investments & Wealth,* January–February 2014, pages 26–28, and Steven Abernathy and Brian Luster, "All in the Family," *Barron's,* March 24, 2014, pages 41–42. Even family portfolios may need special consideration; see Gregory Curtis, "Family-Centric Portfolios," *Private Wealth,* March–April 2014, pages 41–43.

7. Once businesses take root, it's even possible for companies to set up easy and effective retirement plans requiring little in the way of internal costs or administration; see "Operating a SIMPLE IRA Plan," *IRS.gov,* March 15, 2016.

8. Jonathan G. Blattmachr, Mitchell M. Gans, and Diana S.C. Zeydel, "How the Supercharged Credit Shelter Trust^{SM} Avoids the Estate Tax Time Bomb," *Steve Leimberg's Estate Planning Newsletter,* May 16, 2016.

9. There are other techniques that can be used to handle estate costs. For an interesting approach that has the recipient paying the tax, rather than the estate or trust, see Mike Jones and DeeAnn Thompson, "Steinberg v. Commissioner: The Tax Court Cuts the Cord on McCord & Provides Guidance for Net Gift Valuation Discounts," *Steve Leimberg's Estate Planning Newsletter,* October 21, 2015. For another planning approach, see Todd Angkatavanich and James I. Dougherty, "Davidson $320 Million Settlement: Finding Opportunity in Light of the Taxpayer Victory in the Davidson Settlement while Being Mindful of the Uncertainty of CCA 201230033," *Steve Leimberg's Estate Planning Newsletter,* July 14, 2015. For a way to use life insurance and control premium costs, see Lee Slavutin and Richard Harris, "Intergenerational Split Dollar: What We Can Learn from *Morrissette, Levine and Neff,*" *Steve Leimberg's Estate Planning Newsletter,* August 9, 2016. Also see Lee Slavutin, "*Estate of Marion Levine:* Another Intergenerational Split Dollar Ruling by the Tax Court Following the *Morrissette* Decision," *Steve Leimberg's Estate Planning Newsletter,* July 15, 2016. For a time-tested, court-proven approach, see Amy Feldman, "Have-Your-Cake-and-Eat-It Trusts," *Barron's Penta,* November 30, 2015. For another recent key development, see PLR 201614007, which discusses how an incomplete, non-grantor trust (ING) can deliver valuable income tax, gift tax, and estate tax benefits to a family. INGs have particular promise in the right situation with the right assets; see Steven J. Oshins and Brian J. Simmons, "Save State Income Taxes Using a Nevada Incomplete Gift Non-Grantor Trust," *Premier Trust,* October 2014. Another approach that delivers significant value is use of disregarded entities; for information on these and their potential, see Dick Oshins and David A Handler, "Estate Planning With Disregarded Entities," *Steve Leimberg's Estate Planning Newsletter,* December 14, 2015; and Steve Oshins, "1st annual Non-Grantor Trust State Income Tax Chart," *Steve Leimberg's Estate Planning Newsletter,* July 13, 2015. Finally, see Michael D. Weinberg, "A Professional Adviser's Guide to Life Settlements," *Steve Leimberg's Estate Planning Newsletter,* March 24, 2016.

10. Dick Oshins, "PLR 200949012 "Myth—Now You See It, Now You Don't," *Steve Leimberg's Estate Planning Newsletter,* May 31, 2016. This article offers commentary on a highly sophisticated, well-conceived estate-planning tool designed to adhere to the "Control It;

Don't Own It" philosophy, which delivers the control and enjoyment of outright ownership at the same time that it provides shelter from potential litigation.

11. For examples of how far someone can go to waste not, want not, see William D. Lipkind and Terry Prendergast, "New South Dakota Spousal Trust," *Steve Leimberg's Estate Planning Newsletter,* July 7, 2016. Also see Steve Oshins, "2nd Annual Non-Grantor Trust State Income Tax Chart," *Steve Leimberg's Income Tax Planning Newsletter,* July 5, 2016.

12. The legislation that made discounting so attractive in family transfers and distribution has its roots in several places. Among the primary sources are the Revenue Reconciliation Act of 1990, modifications to IRC Sec 2701–2704 effective October 9, 1990, and the Omnibus Budget Reconciliation Act of 1993.

13. For recent commentary on how the IRS and Treasury Department want to modify the rules that make family-discounting techniques so effective in transfer and distribution, see Allyson Versprille and Aaron E. Lorenzo, "Lawmakers Target Spending Bill to Block Estate Tax Rules," *Trusts & Estates,* October 5, 2016. For more technical commentary, see the following: Jonathan G. Blattmachr and Matthew Blattmachr, "Anticipating New Regulations under IRC Section 2704," *Trusts & Estates,* June 4, 2015, and Keith Schiller, "A Call to Congress for Action: Potentially Harmful Impact of 2704 Proposed Regulations on Succession of Family Businesses and Farms and Why It Must be Stopped!" *Steve Leimberg's Estate Planning Newsletter,* September 16, 2016. Also see James G. Blase, "The Future of Discount Planning," *Trusts & Estates,* August 16, 2016, Martin Shenkman, Jonathan G. Blattmachr, Ira S. Herman, and Joy Matak, "Proposed 2704(b) Regulations Will Zap Discounts, Wealthy Taxpayers Should Plan ASAP," *Steven Leimberg's Estate Planning Newsletter,* August 22, 2016, and Ron Aucutt, "Proposed 2704 Regulations Are Significant, But Not a Disaster," *Steve Leimberg's Estate Planning Newsletter,* September 28, 2016. Also see Stephen M. Breitstone and David C. Jacobson, "Estate Planning with Grantor Trusts," *Trusts & Estates,* March 2016, pages 15–23, and Ed Morrow, "Proposed 2704 Regulations' Effect on Basis: Would Higher Valuations Automatically Equal Higher Basis for Those Inheriting a Family Business?" *Steve Leimberg's Estate Planning Newsletter,* October 3, 2016.

14. Recent legislation that made certain previous annual extenders permanent can be found in the Protecting Americans from Tax Hikes Act of 2015, passed on December 18, 2015. For commentary on this legislation, see Julie A. Welch and Cara Smith, "New Law Brings Permanent Tax Changes for Individuals and Businesses," *Journal of Financial Planning,* April 2016, pages 38–40. For a different kind of extension, see PLR 201633012, which provides additional time to make federal estate tax portability election. Finally, for a different kind of deadline, see John Mauldin, "The Bond Rally of a Lifetime,"' *Outside the Box,* August 10, 2016.

15. There has been recent activity concerning securing closing letters from the IRS as pertain to estate tax filings; see Michael Kitces, "New IRS Change Will Require Estates to Request an Estate Closing Letter," *Nerd's Eye View,* September 30, 2015.

16. Chuck Carnevale, "Get Higher Returns and More Dividend Income—in Less Time With Less Risk," *Advisor Perspectives,* June 20, 2016. For an excellent ten-part series on intelligent investing, see The Dividend Guy, "10 Days to Invest with Profits for Life," *The Dividend Guy Blog,* June 2016.

17. As mentioned, leverage used properly can help offset risk. For an introduction to the kinds of investments that can help in this regard, see Canon Hickman, "Alternative Investments Aren't Just for the Rich," *Nasdaq,* May 17, 2016.

18. Another way to secure leverage is to use both favorable tax rates and early tax payments to create long-term, tax-free funds. For an example, see Bruce Steiner, "Using the AMT Sweet Spot for Roth Conversions," *Steve Leimberg's Employee Benefits and Retirement Planning Newsletter,* August 1, 2016. For another approach, see Jamie Hopkins, "Consider a Roth

IRA for Your Client's Emergency Fund to Boost Savings," *Financial Advisor,* October 1, 2016.

19. David J. Yvars Sr., "Consider Combining a CRT with Long-Term Care Insurance," *Trusts & Estates, June 21, 2016.* Also see Landon Jones, "Position Optimization: Allocating across Traditional IRA, Roth IRA, and Non-Qualified Accounts for Higher After-Tax Returns," *Trust Advisor,* June 13, 2016. For clarity on how a basic tool can be used to its maximum advantage, see Ed Morrow and Al Gassman, "Mikel v. Commissioner: Tax Court Approves the Mother of All Crummey Trusts with 60 Beneficiaries," *Steve Leimberg's Estate Planning Newsletter,* May 14, 2015.

20. In some cases taxpayers try to leverage their assets and opportunities by considering more aggressive approaches to housing their assets; for a short review of offshore trusts, see Patricia Donlevy-Rosen, "Offshore Trusts: Why They Work Well," *Steve Leimberg's Asset Protection Planning Newsletter,* September 16, 2015. However, caution must be exercised even when using tools that are regulated more closely to prevent consumer misuse; see Jessica Silver-Greenberg, "Pitfalls of Reverse Mortgages May Pass to Borrower's Heirs," *New York Times/DealBook,* March 26, 2014. Also see Scott Martin, "Advisors Warming to Reverse Mortgages for Mass Market Clients," *Trust Advisor,* August 8, 2016.

21. For potentially high-powered approaches to leverage and compounding, see Al W. King and Pierce McDowell III, "Powerful Private Placement Insurance Strategies with Trusts," *Trusts & Estates,* April 2016, pages 42–49, and Philip Herzberg, "Preserving Lasting Legacies with Dynasty Trusts," *Journal of Financial Planning,* April 2016, pages 34–35.

22. In investing, Dividend Reinvestment Programs (DRIPs) mirror the garden planted one time. For an excellent overview of DRIPs and how they work, see "DRIPs: The Small Investor's Low-Risk Secret to Building Long-Term Wealth," *Moneypaper Publications LLC,* February 2016.

Chapter 9

The Season Schedule

———————◆———————

Prologue

n my experience, players who master the game of Wealth Transfer and Distribution manage the season schedule with skill and foresight. Since a player's game can end on any given day, players need to think ahead and put their thoughts into action. We can't expect to have time to wrap up our efforts; we need to be prepared to tally our score at any time![1]

John is one of the finest individuals I know, and he has been one of my favorite clients for years. He is conscientious about always being prepared for his game to end—which has become more challenging in recent years, as he has gotten older. Since his wife, Jenny, is in declining health, and since his own capacities are being tested by age, John has concluded that he needs more help than he once did. For this reason, he has asked one of his sons to play a greater part in his game.

Until recently John was the classic family patriarch; his wife and all their children looked to him as the final decision maker. Like many patriarchs and matriarchs, John was always ready to take whatever measures were necessary to address problems or needs that arose, without consulting or involving other family members unless necessary. With the passage of time, however, John came to realize that he couldn't manage everything on his own anymore.

Faced with growing limitations, and unwilling to drop the full responsibility on one of his children without preparation or forewarning, John decided to make sure that his son Ted was ready to step in when it was time for John to step out.

As his first action, John shared the family's financial information with Ted. In many families, sharing financial information is uncomfortable, and even unnerving. But by making this information available to Ted, John took the first step in bringing his family into the conversation.

Next, John made sure his team understood that Ted was becoming a key player. He set up meetings with his key advisors to build Ted's knowledge of the family's finances and plans. This started a disclosure process that went beyond dollars and cents: John wanted Ted to understand not only what John and his wife had, but also what they planned to do. Once this process was complete, John broached the most important subject: *why he and Jenny had chosen to do what they were doing.*

By taking Ted into his confidence, John changed the family dynamic. Once Ted understood his parents' choices, it became easier to bring the remaining children into the conversation. For parents, one of the greatest challenges in our game is making their wishes known and understood. Since John and Jenny had different transfer plans for each child, it was incumbent upon John to explain this during his lifetime rather than letting it become known only after his death. When one child receives his inheritance directly while another receives it in trust, the risk of confusion and hurt feelings is high unless some explanation is provided.[2] Within a year's time, John had explained his objectives to the entire family. But this was only the first step. To make sure that his and Jenny's wishes would be understood and honored, John took another step: He asked the children to become active participants in certain aspects of his game.

John and Jenny shared a strong disposition toward charitable giving. After years of dealing directly with charities, John decided to bring Ted into the process, effectively making him the new family representative to these charities. Ted's new responsibilities enabled him to understand why John and

Jenny had chosen the charities they did, and showed him how the family's donations could best be used to help others.

At the same time, John made sure that Ted learned from the family's advisors *how* he and Jenny had played the game over the years. Before Ted could fully understand where his parents were, he needed to understand how they had gotten there. Once Ted understood what was important to John and Jenny and how their actions reflected these priorities, he better appreciated their goals. While John was grooming Ted to assume primary responsibility for the family's finances, he also wanted to make sure Ted shared his and Jenny's values.

When John turned eighty-five, satisfied with Ted's mastery of his new role, he advised Ted and his siblings that he and Jenny were resigning as custodians of their trust, and were appointing Ted to serve as their successor. At the same time, John decided to provide the other two children, Matt and Laura, with the same education he had given their older brother, in order to ensure that the family had skilled and knowledgeable backups in case anything were to happen to Ted. By doing this, he made sure that there would be no shortage of ready players to step up to the plate if the need arose (recall our discussion of bench strength in chapter 7).

As it turned out, John and Jenny continued to thrive, and they are in fairly good health even to this day. However, the defensive steps they took by ensuring that all their children are prepared to address family matters have secured peace of mind for them. Rather than placing the entire burden on Ted's shoulders, they have made it possible for the whole family to participate. Each of the children has a role, and they perform these roles with the full confidence and trust of their parents. John and Jenny don't worry whether the children can work together because the children have demonstrated their ability to do so ever since it was asked of them. And when something finally does happen to John and Jenny, each player in the family will know and embrace his or her role in the family's affairs.

John's foresight in managing the season schedule has had another major impact: His thoughtful approach has inspired his children to duplicate his efforts within their own families by sharing information and responsibility with their own children. As a result, three generations of the family are making sure that if one player is taken from the field at any time, there are ample skilled and ready substitutes waiting to play the game.

Because the game of Wealth Transfer and Distribution is both open-ended and finite, it is necessary to anticipate whatever can happen. As players we must be ready to be taken from the game at a moment's notice; at the same time, we must be equally ready to jump into the middle of someone else's game. It is essential to understand that there are multiple games being played at any given time that may require us to take on different roles. Given these demands, the importance of having our personal game under control should be clear. Thus, managing the season schedule is vital.

The Championship

While many games can be played on an ad hoc basis, the game of Wealth Transfer and Distribution has a finite time frame: the player's lifetime. With a finite schedule, we must realize that there are at least four periods to our game: preseason, regular season, postseason, and championship. In my opinion, the easiest period of the playing season to understand is the championship, so let's examine that first.

The championship game tells the player how well she did; it provides the final tally of results. The only problem with the championship game is that in many cases, the player isn't alive to know the outcome. The championship game generally captures the final actions of the player, telling us how effectively and efficiently she transferred and distributed her wealth, whether by will, trust, or other device. It also tells us, when appropriate, how well we managed the tax authorities. Since this outcome is tied to the player's death, it naturally follows that the last points scored by the player aren't tallied until she is gone.[3]

Obviously, the fact that we cannot know whether we've actually succeeded doesn't stop us from playing the game. But many players don't fully appreciate that it *is* possible to predict the likely outcome, even if we can't know everything down to the last detail. For this to happen, the player needs to allocate time and effort to the other parts of the season schedule.

When this is done, the predictability of our results increases. Thus, while the championship is the most easily understood "game" of the season, everything we do in the earlier periods (preseason, regular season, and postseason) leads directly to this final tally.

Although in many games the outcome is dependent on how we perform in the last few minutes (or even seconds) of the contest, in *our* game the result of the championship is best understood as the result of multiple prior events. The planning and preparation of earlier periods directly affects our performance in the championship. When the game of Wealth Transfer and Distribution is played well, it is often possible to predict the outcome before it actually happens. In the course of my career I have been able to help more than a few clients predict what was going to happen after their deaths; this knowledge provided them with peace of mind and enabled their heirs to focus on their emotional needs rather than on their financial concerns.[4]

It's common to hear athletes talk about having fun before the most important game of their lives; they do this because they know they are so well prepared that victory is a foregone conclusion (at least in their minds). Therefore, all that is left for them to do is to execute . . . and to have fun doing so. In the game of Wealth Transfer and Distribution, the most fun a player can have is to achieve the sense of satisfaction that stems from knowing your preparation has made victory inevitable. To see how we get to this position, we need to consider the three other periods in our season schedule: preseason preparation, regular-season games, and playoffs.

The Preseason

Preseason planning is the first step toward championship victory. In almost every game, there is a time for conditioning and preparation. This is the preseason.

Preseason preparation in the game of Wealth Transfer and Distribution is no different. This is the time when the player decides what kind of game he wants to play, and consequently, what he needs to field the appropriate team. To this end, the player defines his goals and the objectives that must be achieved in order to reach them. The player's desired outcome dictates what he must do in order to win the game. In some cases, objectives have time restrictions imposed upon them; in other cases, the player is free to choose when the game starts, and sometimes when it ends.

Preseason activities should include consideration of everything we have discussed up to this point:

◊   Defining the Game
◊   Understanding the Rules and the Playing Field
◊   Building Your Team
◊   Keeping Score
◊   Defense
◊   Offense

Defining the Game and Assembling Your Team in the Preseason

Preseason is when the player focuses on the mechanics of his intent, and defining goals and objectives during the preseason is critical. In addition to settling on what he wants to accomplish, the player must identify what interim objectives must be met in order to achieve these larger goals.

Since the game of Wealth Transfer and Distribution can last decades, the player's ability to support the cost of the game she chooses to play is paramount. Assume for the moment that our player embarks on a game designed to move assets to her children over thirty years. To accomplish this, first and foremost, the player must live that long. Second, not only must she be able to support the cost of playing the game, she must also be able to absorb the loss of the value that these assets would otherwise have delivered to her. Finally, she must allow for the possibility that changes to any number of rules and regulations could alter the playing field more than a few times over the years. This type of game cries out for detailed preparation and discipline.

To field the best team possible, the player needs to take into account the considerations we discussed in previous chapters: the rules and regulations, her desired playing field, and the most appropriate defensive and offensive schemes. If the player's team is assembled with these factors in mind, that outcome is more likely to be achieved. It is also necessary to remember that any player can have a number of preseasons; for each discrete regular-season game the player decides to play, a new set of preseason activities should be undertaken.[5]

Scorekeeping

There is another important reason to use your preseason time to carefully build your team: scorekeeping. While any lost or poorly played game is frustrating, the frustration is magnified when neither the players nor their beneficiaries are even aware that more could have been done. Unlike many conventional games, in which it is obvious when bad plays stop a team's progress, in the game of Wealth Transfer and Distribution, there are no natural indicators of what could have been. In golf, for example, the player plays against par. Playing to par is an achievement that few golfers ever experience, no matter how long they play the game. Likewise, few players shoot par in our Wealth Transfer and Distribution game. However—and this is a significant consideration—in our game, there is no scorecard against which to evaluate our scores. The only way a player knows how much better he or she could have played is by consulting with managers, coaches, and specialists to see what else could have been done.[6]

Since objective measurement is often unsatisfying or difficult to accomplish, most players never realize the opportunities they have left behind or problems they have created. How can this be addressed? By making use of specialists *while playing the game*. Given the difficulties of understanding and interpreting rules and regulations, playing environments, timing issues, and changes in scoring, the casual player, especially in preseason, should seek assistance to ensure that his basic decisions are sound. Even the most ardent do-it-yourselfer can benefit from a second opinion.

Today, the practice of getting a second opinion is common; most patients secure a second medical point of view before having surgery. And yet, amazingly, many people neglect this same step when making equally important financial decisions. All too often individuals go it alone rather than taking the time to challenge their assumptions by seeking expert advice. The housing debacle of 2006–2007 is a great example of a situation in which second opinions would have helped. How many people might have saved themselves time, money, and pain by making sure that the homes they bought and the mortgages they used were appropriate to their circumstances? Literally millions! Interestingly, the rules changed in the aftermath of the housing bubble; before an elderly homeowner can take on a reverse mortgage today, he or she must participate in an interview with a third-party counselor.[7] Perhaps a similar interview would help first-time homebuyers avoid making mistakes with lifelong consequences.

The Right Tools

Before the game can begin, the player must have the right tools. In addition to knowing *what* we want to do and *when* we want to do it, we must know *what we need to have* in order to get it done. Without the proper equipment, the player's ability to participate is impeded. In simple games, preparation can be basic. Imagine a softball game at a family picnic: For this game to be played, there are a limited number of necessary steps. We must make sure that we have the right equipment (ball, bat, gloves); we need the right environment (a patch of land suitable for our purposes); and we need enough willing participants to warrant the effort. If any of these components are missing, the game may not occur; it's difficult to play softball without a ball or bat. In more complicated games, there will be more pieces to gather before we can play.

In our game, the same is true. Whether it's money, borrowing capacity, cash flow, savings, or some other financial measure, unless we have what we need, we shouldn't play the game. Having the desire or even the will to play isn't enough; the successful player must have the necessary means and wherewithal. Essentially, you shouldn't play if you can't pay![8]

Game Scheduling and Timing

Different games have different goals, and different objectives must be met in order to achieve them. For example, imagine a game based on the timing of events. This would be similar to a trick play in football in which the quarterback hands the ball off to a runner, only to receive it back in order to make a pass downfield. This play is effectively a smaller game within a larger game, and in order for it to work, timing is essential. If any part breaks down—that is, if any player fails to perform the right action at the right time—the play will fail. And due to the multiple moving parts, that danger exists even under the best of circumstances.

Consider the situation described in chapter 8, in which a player over 70½ wants to make a charitable donation directly from his IRA account during a tax-extender period. To complete this transaction, a lot of things must happen within a very short time. Before the law became permanent in 2016, if there were any breakdown, this play would not work, and the small game would be lost.[9] This is a good example of how timing is important if we are to accomplish our goals. Making sure that every aspect of this transaction is understood and implemented requires meticulous preseason planning and care.

Next, we need to determine when certain important games should be scheduled. Let's consider annual gifts, for example: Annual gifts must be completed during a calendar year if they are to meet the objective of using the player's annual gift exclusion. Assume our player has four children and six grandchildren, and wishes to give $14,000 to each of these individuals. In order to play this game, the player must have $140,000 available. Again, we must have our pieces in place; without these funds, the question of timing is moot.

Even with funds in hand, however, there are obstacles to overcome. Starting this game on December 25 requires a significant amount of last-minute preparation and coordination. Gifting $140,000 by December 31 is not as simple as writing checks. While the game begins with fund identification and check writing, it ends only when the checks are deposited in the beneficiaries' accounts! Thus, even in this relatively simple game, planning, executing, and timing the endgame requires several discrete actions. I have seen these gifts fail more than once: Children forgot to deposit the checks; gifts were mislaid; parents "held" the checks for their children; checks were thrown out with the Christmas cards, etc. Make no mistake: When it comes to gifting, there are many ways for the best intentions to come to naught.

By contrast, consider the same player who makes a series of gifts at death. In this case, the calendar for completion is wide open and subject to change only when the player dies. Here, time is not the issue; the real issue is gathering and distribution—making sure that adequate assets exist at death to satisfy the wish, and then following through by ensuring that the gifts are distributed to the right people.

Nevertheless, here too, there is plenty that can go wrong. I have seen clients give away assets they no longer own: For example, Bill wanted to give his '65 Mustang to his nephew, Walter. Unfortunately, Bill's widow sold this car while Bill was sick because the family needed money. Terry wanted to make a gift to his grammar school, but by the time of his death, the Catholic Archdiocese of Chicago had closed the school due to falling attendance. Mary wanted to make a direct cash gift to her niece, Emily, for college; regrettably, however, Emily is only five years old and can't accept the gift!

Obviously, not all attempts at gifting need to end this way. The point is that making sure you can do what you want to do, whether during your life or at death, requires more than simply the desire and the ability; it also demands planning. It's not enough to *want* to do something: Deliberate, considered action must follow, and this is why preseason activity lays the groundwork for success—and the earlier you start, the better.[10] Given that multiple regular-season games can be played, it stands to reason that there must be multiple preseason activities. The accomplished player is likely to be starting preseason preparation for one game at the same time that she is finishing another, earlier game. Unfortunately, many players limit themselves to one preseason, or just a few. By doing this, the player prevents herself from playing as many games as possible.

National statistics indicate that many players never engage in *any* preseason activities. These are the players who do nothing, and let the rules and regulations determine their outcomes for them. In 2016, it is estimated that as many as 60 percent of all Americans don't have the most basic planning tool, a will.[11] If true, this means that at least 60 percent of all potential players have not given serious consideration to preseason activities. We all know it is wise to warm up before strenuous exercise; whether we are running a sprint or a marathon, it makes good sense to stretch, to prepare for what we are about to do if we want to finish without injury. In the game of Wealth Transfer and Distribution, getting ready means setting the stage for action, and it is necessary for success.

By now, the need for preseason activity should be apparent. It marks that time when we choose the game to be played; determine what coaches, managers, and specialists we need; consider what rules and regulations are going to affect our efforts; and evaluate the effects of the playing environment on our game. Whether the game is long or short, complicated or simple, the player needs not only to be ready to play the game, but also to have energy and resources in reserve if the game becomes more demanding than originally expected. Showing up to play the game without prior preparation is a recipe for defeat and frustration.

And yet despite the overwhelming benefits of preseason training, many players forgo it and simply show up to play, ignoring the benefits of preseason actions and moving directly into regular-season games. When this happens, the player seldom gets what he wants.[12] By not making use of the preseason, the player starts his games cold. This is playing on the run. It's similar to changing shoes in the parking lot, gathering golf clubs, and rushing to the first tee to play golf—a hurried approach that usually costs the player a few strokes over the first several holes. Until a good rhythm is established, the player is apt to be playing *at* golf as opposed to *playing golf.*

Similar outcomes occur in the game of Wealth Transfer and Distribution. When a player decides to start the game without consideration for preparation, what generally follows is planning on the fly, as opposed to purposeful planning. Execution generally suffers, and success is unlikely. But a truly effective set of preseason activities, undertaken with the expert assistance of a specialist (as recommended earlier),[13] puts the player in a position to win the regular-season games.

The Regular Season

Regular-season games take place at various times during a player's lifetime. These games occur when the player decides to take an action that will yield an advantage or benefit. In some cases, only transfer will occur; in others, both transfer and distribution take place. When these regular-season games are well conceived, not only do they accomplish something in the here and now, but they also set the tone for both postseason and championship games. In other words, regular-season games serve as bridges between the preseason and the ultimate results the player wants to achieve.[14]

The player who has the necessary resources to play early and often can more easily secure his desired outcome. Regular-season games build the foundation for the player's long-term goals, whatever they may be, and demonstrate the effectiveness of the player's efforts. Why is this important?

While it is possible to skip preseason, regular season, and postseason activities, it is much easier for the player to win when he goes through the entire process. Where preseason planning ensures that the player is ready to play, the next step—putting in place the legal devices necessary for transfer and distribution—puts the player more firmly on the road to ultimate success. This is regular-season play. By translating preseason plans into regular-season experiences and victories, the player insulates himself against disappointment and failure in the event that the postseason arrives before he is ready. He also gets to refine his plans during the course of these regular-season games, making them more adaptable to changes in tax or legal environments as they occur.

The number and timing of regular-season games varies among players. There is no set number. It has been my experience, however, that most accomplished players play a great number of regular-season games. Why? Because no matter how thorough the player's preseason planning may have been, reality alters our expected results once that planning is put into action.[15]

For example, assume our player wants to make cash gifts to her children. Her expectation is that her kids will use these gifts wisely, and she conducts her preseason planning accordingly. When the regular season arrives, however, some of the children meet her expectations while others fritter away her gifts. In a sense, our player can be said to have lost an early regular-season game, and she may therefore want to make a change to her subsequent gifts. For example, she might give to some children (the ones who used their money wisely) but not to others (those who didn't). Or, alternatively, she may make some gifts directly but place conditions on others to prevent their misuse. In a case like this, the player makes an adjustment when intent meets the real world. This is one of the advantages of early regular-season games; they serve to confirm or invalidate expectations.[16]

Why is this important? Because it may be much easier to digest a small disappointment than a larger one. If this disappointment had occurred in a postseason or championship game (say, for example, that she had left a third of her fortune to a feckless child who squandered it), the failure of our player's children to live up to her expectations could have been a great shock, and potentially one from which her game might not have recovered. Better the small shock than the larger one.

Similarly, multiple regular-season games help the player understand herself. These lower-stakes games help the player determine what feels right. Our player may discover that giving is harder than she'd imagined, for whatever reason, and this additional information may guide her future actions. By playing multiple games in her regular season, the player learns more about the game and its effects on her, and this knowledge makes her a better player.[17]

Despite the obvious advantages of having more regular-season games than not, many players are nonetheless inclined to play the game only once, or as few times as possible. Sometimes outside influences affect the player's ability to play. Some players die early; others don't have much to transfer or distribute. Some become disabled and need to keep what they have for themselves. In other words, a variety of exogenous events can thwart a player's opportunity to learn how to play the game better. When coupled with the fact that many players make no effort to play at all, this means that the majority of players are dangerously unprepared for the games that really matter.

The Playoffs—Welcome to Postseason!

In sports, making it to the postseason generally means that the quality of play during the regular season was high and you had a winning team. The same is true in the game of Wealth Transfer and Distribution; not every team makes it to the playoffs. In fact, the percentage of players who qualify for postseason play in *our* game is far lower than in the sports we follow. For example, in baseball, five teams in each league qualify for postseason play, and in basketball, the Eastern and Western Conferences each send eight teams to the NBA Playoffs. In college football, postseason play is marked by participation in a bowl game—an honor bestowed upon more than 50 percent of all contending teams.

In the game of Wealth Transfer and Distribution, postseason play is marked by final actions, which reflect a player's focused efforts. In other words, planning must be purposeful and directed. For this reason, few players qualify for postseason events because their actions are restricted either by law or regulation. For example, let's suppose I die without a will. I live in California, and California has a plan for the transfer and distribution of my assets, irrespective of whether I am rich or poor.[18] That fact that I am married restricts my options even further, as California law has something to say about the distribution of assets in cases in which no beneficiaries are named. In the case of my 401(k) plan or my IRA, there is a predetermined endgame based on my marital or family situation. By failing to play an easy regular-season game—leaving a will—I have subjected myself to a winnowing process that eliminates many players, either because they choose not to play in the first place or because they make too few of their regular-season games count.[19]

Finally, in those cases in which only the most basic planning is done, players actually impose their own limitations. Consider our earlier example of a player who made a regular-season game of reevaluating her gifts to her children, some of whom had frittered away the money she'd given them; now imagine leaving all your money in one lump sum to an impulsive child who takes it to the racetrack. Given how often players make these kinds of mistakes, you might think that postseason play requires either high-value assets or difficult, complex planning. Neither of these assumptions is true.

Postseason play in our Wealth Transfer and Distribution game depends on the understanding that our game need not end with death. In other words, it is possible to have a second opportunity to remedy lifetime oversights or missed chances.[20] As I mentioned before, if an earlier gift to a child turned out to be waste of money, future gifts can be eliminated entirely or modified so that the child has enjoyment but not ownership of the gift. Similarly, if the player finds that his wealth exceeds his original expectations, he can expand his gifts to charity or give money to friends who need it. In most sports, postseason play requires regular-season success, but in our Wealth Transfer and Distribution game, a player's team can secure a postseason berth by taking the time either to alter certain decisions or to postpone them until a later date—possibly after the player's death, or even after multigenerational deaths.

———— ♦ ————

Those players who reach the postseason view this level of play as the most desirable. Here they get to play the game at its highest level. When I advise clients, our goal is always to reach postseason play. We don't want our championship game to be a regular-season game played once. And when played at the highest level, postseason games often evolve into true championship activity. Sadly, few players reach this pinnacle of success in playing the game because they limit themselves. Players who get to the championship round of play take their postseason play and elevate it yet again. Players who reach this degree of sophistication and ability are generally prepared to play *any* opponent.

Given that opponents in championship matches can be diverse (championship games generally pit the player against legal and tax authorities at multiple levels), it is vital for the player to understand what kind of opponent he faces. In fact, it is fair to say that the true championship game is a multiple-game setting, just as a chess master might play a series of simultaneous games against multiple opponents. Victory at this level is a thrill, and it marks an accomplishment for any player. It is a reward reserved for those who play the game as it was truly intended to be played.

———— ♦ ————

Here's an example of postseason play leading to championship season results. Recently I met with a family whose matriarch had used her Limited Power of Appointment to alter a trust created by her parents in the late 1960s (this power had been granted to her at the time the document was drafted). The changes she made modified the final distribution of assets to provide her children with enjoyment of those assets and income during their lifetimes . . . but to pass final ownership to her grandchildren. This means that a document drafted almost fifty years ago may not be finalized until eighty years from now or more—a transfer and distribution plan lasting over 130 years!

At the same time, her children who already benefitted from parental gifts decided to make generation-skipping gifts of their own, moving assets from themselves to their children and grandchildren. In this case, the gifts took the form of a commercial property with low lease rates guaranteed for the next fifty years. This would enable the children to use the low value driven by these prolonged leases as the starting point for their gifts. What is important here is that this property is likely to be worth many times its lease value when the extensions stop. In this case, these parents are giving up modest cash flow for the next fifty years in order to deliver a downstream benefit of millions of dollars to their children and grandchildren.

The best-played games are often weighted toward preseason and regular-season activities. Since these are the foundations of a well-played game, it is necessary to highlight them. By making preseason planning and regular-season games the focus of effort, players put themselves in the position to play in the postseason, and sometimes, in championship games. In short, there is nothing like planning well and executing early.

It would be wonderful if every player were able to experience the excitement of making it through the regular season. As I noted, however, for various reasons, most players either don't or choose not to. There are numerous reasons this may occur: ignorance, disinterest, laziness, and even spite. It is my opinion, however, that every player who chooses to play should play as if the game being played is the last one. Care and consideration should be taken at all times. While we all would like a second bite of the apple, few of us ever have that opportunity. The smart player plans carefully in the preseason, plays the game at hand as if it were his last, and gives it 100 percent.

Notes

1. This chapter serves as a summation of the concepts and ideas explored in the previous chapters. It looks back on the strategies and tactics explored so far and puts them to work. As a result, there are fewer issues to consider; for this reason, the endnotes for this chapter will be fewer in number and more casual. To the extent there are comments, these comments will address ways in which players can take advantage of concessions offered by court cases, legislative action, and/or tax rulings that affect the season schedule.

2. Many families are now incorporating "letters of intent" into their planning processes. These letters, written by the parents, accompany estate documents and help family members understand *why* certain actions are taken. Letters of intent are informal documents that guide the process and clarify parental intent. To learn how and why letters of intent can be of value, see UBS, "8 Facts About How Families Need Look at Inheritance Now," *Forbes*, November 7, 2016.

3. Whenever a person dies, there is usually some distributive process. When the deceased has significant value, this process can incorporate both transfer and distribution aspects, the difference being that transfer carries a tax impact, whereas distribution generally avoids tax (see chapter 2).

4. Most sophisticated financial planners, attorneys, and accountants have software that allows them to predict outcomes based on multiple factors. While the most common desire is to see what everyone is going to get, one of the most important applications tells us whether we will achieve what we want. The significant difference between achieving what we want and seeing what everyone is going to get is the difference between effectiveness and efficiency.

5. Preseason activities can change on a dime. When Donald Trump upset Hillary Clinton in the 2016 presidential race, a number of preseason assumptions went out the window. For noteworthy comments, see Jonathan G. Blattmachr and Martin Shenkman, "Trump Wins, Republicans Control House & Senate, A Brave New World for Estate Planners," *Steve Leimberg's Estate Planning Newsletter*, November 10, 2016, and Suzanne L. Shier and Benjamin J. Lavin, "Tax and Wealth Planning Implications of a Trump Presidency," *WealthManagement.com*, November 9, 2016. Despite Trump's surprise victory, preseason planning in future years may well be dominated by the question of family valuation discounts. For a current overview of what should be addressed, see Mark R. Parthemer, "Section 2704 Proposed Regs: Action Steps for High Net Worth Families Despite the Confusion," *Trusts & Estates*, October 24, 2016.

6. Distributing assets is one of the primary goals of a successful transfer plan, but it is equally important to know that our efforts to distribute our wealth have worked. Historically, taxpayers knew that they could make final distributions when the IRS provided them with a Closing Letter; in recent times, however, the IRS has switched from Estate Tax Closing Letters to Transcripts. For information on this change, see Chuck Rubin, "Using Transcripts in Lieu of Estate Closing Letters," *Steve Leimberg's Estate Planning Newsletter*, January 13, 2016. Along the same lines, we need to know that creditor claims have been satisfied; for a change that settles this question for Florida residents, see George Karibjanian and Jonathan Galler, "Jones v. Golden: As to the Limitations Period for Reasonably Ascertainable Creditor's Claims, Literally (Almost Finally) Means Literally," *Steve Leimberg's Estate Planning Newsletter*, October 5, 2015.

7. For a thorough and clear overview on reverse mortgages, see "Reverse Mortgages," *Federal Trade Commission,* June 2015. To learn how help sometimes comes from the most peculiar places, see Lark Blanche Christerson, "The Highway Trust Fund," *Deutsche Bank,* August 31, 2015. In this newsletter, the author describes how a short-term patch for the Highway Trust Fund carried with it a handful of important tax provisions on matters as diverse as mortgage reporting, expanded statutes of limitations when basis is overstated, and even tax return due dates.

8. For a handy guide that summarizes whether we have the right equipment and have considered the correct issues, see Raymond James, "Check This List—Twice—Before Year-End," *Financial Perspectives,* Fall 2016.

9. For a clear understanding of our new world as relates to charitable gifts from IRA accounts, see Conrad Teitell, "Meet Dec. 31 Deadline for Tax-Free Direct Charitable/IRA Distributions," *WealthManagement.com,* November 6, 2016.

10. The same is true for accumulation activities as well. Knowing when to take action is critical if we are going to grow what we have; see "Do You Know When IS the Right Time to Buy a Stock?" *Dividend Monk,* April 26, 2015.

11. For a clear explanation of why planning is necessary, see Patrick Carlson, "Why Attorneys Need to Discuss Estate Planning with All Clients," *WealthManagement.com,* November 7, 2016, and "What Do Americans Think About Estate Planning?" *WealthCounsel,* Fall 2016.

12. For an overview of how a small mistake can lead to an undesirable consequence, see Lorraine New, "Field Attorney Advice 20152201F," *Steve Leimberg's Estate Planning Newsletter,* September 10, 2015. This article illustrates what happens when gifts are not adequately disclosed, even if the three-year statute of limitations has elapsed. For an interesting look at what happens when carelessness rules the day, see Paul Hood, "IRS Field Attorney Advice 20152201F: Documentation on Gift Tax Return Did Not Rise to the Level of Disclosure Required to Trigger Statute of Limitations," *Steve Leimberg's Estate Planning Newsletter,* October 1, 2015.

13. Specialists who prepare their players well are worth their weight in gold; see Owen Fiore, "Steinberg v. Commissioner: Agreement to Assume Potential Estate Tax Liability in Determining Fair Market Value of a Gift," *Steve Leimberg's Estate Planning Newsletter,* September 15, 2015. When proper planning is employed, the outcome can be financially and emotionally gratifying!

14. It must be noted that not all games are voluntary. One of the more common regular-season games for almost everyone is income tax filing. For many people, filing an income tax return is fairly simple; however, there are times when even income tax filings become challenging, and that challenge can result in the need for an amended return. Whether to amend is a matter that deserves careful consideration. See Tom Herman, "You Made a Mistake on Your Tax Return. Should You Amend It?" *The Wall Street Journal,* October 23, 2016.

15. Money and health concerns dominate regular and postseason play; as a result, marking accomplishments as we go helps us in the long run. Failure to do so can lead to bigger problems; see James Schiavone, "Running Out of Money Is Top Retirement Concern, Says AICPA Survey of Financial Planners," *AICPA,* October 6, 2016. Also see American Funds, "Retirement Income," *Seeking Alpha,* September 27, 2016, Lance Roberts, "Don't Blame 'Baby Boomers' for Not Retiring," *Seeking Alpha,* September 27, 2016, and Suzanne Woolley, "You Risk a Ragged Retirement if You're Counting on These Numbers," *WealthManangement.com,* November 1, 2016.

16. While multiple games can hone your skills and make you a better player, it is essential to understand that each game gives the IRS the opportunity to check your work. Understanding the options available to the IRS and limits they are subject to is helpful.

See Robert W. Wood, "The IRS Can Audit for Three Years, Six . . . or Forever," *Forbes*, December 15, 2014.

17. One of the most common-regular season activities is qualified plan rollovers. This occurs when a player moves money from a pension plan or some other type of retirement plan like a 401(k) plan into an IRA Rollover account. It should be noted that in the past, the IRS has been very strict in its interpretation of the rules; however, a self-certification procedure enacted in 2016 has made correcting mistakes a little easier. See Jon Vogler, "IRS Provides Relief for Certain Savers Who Miss Rollover Deadline," *Advisor Perspectives*, November 7, 2016.

18. "Dying Without a Will in California," Californiatrusts.com.

19. It's even possible to back into predetermined endgames. For example, see what happens when required minimum distributions on a Roth IRA fail to occur. Information Letter 2016-0071 addresses the consequences of failing to take minimum required distributions of a Roth IRA under the Life-Expectancy Rule. Also see Dawn S. Markowitz, "Inherited IRA Distributions Treated as Taxable," *Trusts & Estates*, October 20, 2016.

20. The taxpayer in the Davidson case (see chapter 8, endnote 9) enjoyed a significant tax victory, but that didn't stop the estate from looking for even more benefit; see Jonathan G. Blattmachr, Mitchell Gans, and Diana S. Zeydel, "Davidson v. Deloitte: The Davidson Estate Sues Deloitte Over 'SCIN in GRAT' Strategy," *Steve Leimberg's Estate Planning Newsletter*, October 7, 2015.

Chapter 10
Fouls and Penalties

———————◆———————

Prologue

t's difficult to recount our mistakes; no one likes to dredge up bad experiences more than they have to. This is certainly true in the game of Wealth Transfer and Distribution. But the opportunity to learn from mistakes presents itself most plainly when things go wrong in a big way, as the following example illustrates.

I once inherited a set of circumstances under which the best possible outcome would be to stop the bleeding. Barbara came to me for help after the sudden death of her second husband, Mortie, who had controlled the couple's financial lives. Unfortunately, Mortie's view of compliance was flawed, to say the very least. He regularly understated his and Barbara's taxable income and artificially boosted their deductions when filing their annual tax returns. He used excessive discounts when making gifts of illiquid assets to his son Harold, who ran the family business, in an attempt to "fool the bastards" in Washington. He actively sought out pension plan strategies that promised him disproportionate benefit. In other words, wherever there was the opportunity to push the envelope or to cross the lines, Mortie acted with reckless abandon.

Barbara was what the IRS refers to as an "innocent spouse"; like too many spouses, she signed whatever forms put in front of her without question or review. She believed Mortie when he told her that all was well. When he died, however, she discovered some horrifying truths. Mortie's estate was large enough that Barbara was obligated to file an estate return, and when she did, Mortie's dubious dealings came to light.[1]

The first discovery was his effort to hand over 50 percent of the family business to Harold for $1. Since the business was worth more than $5 million, the IRS rightfully claimed that Mortie had made a disguised gift of almost $2.5 million to Harold.[2] While this action did not precipitate an immediate tax, it was the red flag that prompted the IRS to conduct a full-blown tax audit of the estate return . . . and this audit created havoc for Barbara and her family.

Once the IRS discovered the undervaluation in the sale of the business interest, they initiated a thorough review of Mortie's actions over the previous twenty years. Because fraud is an open-ended audit event that can be prosecuted years later, Barbara found herself trying to defend actions of which she had been utterly ignorant . . . and she lacked even the simplest evidence of her innocence[3] (this underscores the importance of knowing where backup materials are stored and how to access them). By the time the IRS finished the first stage of its audit process, Barbara found herself owing the government more than $1 million in unpaid gift taxes, including interest and penalties. But this was only the beginning.

As a second step, the IRS began reviewing Mortie and Barbara's income tax filings over the past twenty years. Again, Mortie's overly aggressive actions had created significant problems for Barbara. One of Mortie's dealings involved his retirement plan, which promised benefits to Mortie and Barbara that were unsupported by the Tax Code. The plan deductions were deemed abusive, and as a result, not only were they disallowed, but penalties and back interest were applied as well. When the IRS finished its review, which resulted in the disqualification of the retirement plan in its entirety, Barbara faced a $4 million tax bill including penalties, interest, and back taxes.[4]

But the IRS was not finished yet. Because evidence of fraud was rampant, agents began looking at other actions Mortie had taken over the years, and Barbara soon found herself responsible for unreported income of more than $5 million—a discovery that cost her still *more* in taxes. To meet these bills,

Barbara was forced to sell assets—which generated even more tax obligations to the government, since her sales created capital gains. Every time she sold an asset, she triggered another taxable event. By the time she'd finished, the total cost of removing the IRS from her doorstep was staggering: nearly $10 million.[5]

Barbara's experience was painful in other ways: She lost her lifestyle, she was forced to sell her home, and her health was affected. Barbara paid a heavy price for Mortie's actions; she lost nearly everything that she and Mortie had acquired. When she finally resolved her affairs, she was almost broken and very bitter. Happily, in the years that followed, she adjusted to a simpler and less expensive lifestyle. Today, she lives modestly, secure in the knowledge that her past problems are over and her future has potential.[6]

Needless to say, failing to understand Mortie's actions was the worst thing that ever happened to Barbara.

The lesson to be learned from this story is that every person must understand his or her tax responsibility; it should be clear that innocence or ignorance can provide little defense when things go wrong. Moreover, it is essential for couples to share the responsibility for tax compliance.

There would also be a lesson here for Mortie, were he alive to learn it. Whenever possible, I encourage clients and friends to measure the potential benefits of pushing the limits against the risks of conflict with governing authorities. In the game of Wealth Transfer and Distribution, avoiding fouls and penalties should be a principal goal.[7]

The Consequences of Breaking the Rules

Every game imposes consequences when rules are broken. In some cases, the offending team suffers a penalty (e.g., the loss of a down, or a basket disallowed), while in other instances, the opposing team enjoys a benefit (e.g., additional yards awarded for holding, or an automatic first down). In the game of Wealth Transfer and Distribution, the impact of fouls and the imposition of penalties are no different.

In basketball, fouls are categorized according to severity. *Personal* fouls are the least severe, and may even be inadvertent (accidental contact is among the most common of these fouls); *technical* fouls tend to involve unsportsmanlike conduct; *flagrant* fouls, such as excessive contact that risks injury to the other player, are grounds for ejection from the game.

A player who commits five personal fouls is disqualified from additional play. A player who commits technical fouls can incur additional repercussions, such as free throws for the other team, game disqualification, and even fines. Flagrant fouls can lead to immediate disqualification, even before reaching five fouls. In other words, an offense of greater magnitude can result in earlier disqualification and more adverse outcomes than what would occur in the course of normal play.

The same is true in Wealth Transfer and Distribution. The further one gets from the letter and spirit of the game, the more punitive the outcome. It is also possible to take a marginally defensible position and turn it into an extreme and blatant disregard of the rules and regulations. This happens most often when the player acts as if rules either don't exist or don't apply to him.[8]

Where tax matters are concerned, fraud generally results in the worst possible penalties. Fraud can lead not only to additional taxes, but also to penalties, interest, and even jail time. This doesn't mean, however, that a minor event can't lead to a disastrous outcome. For example, if one accidentally disqualifies a retirement account, it is possible for the worst possible tax outcome to occur: immediate taxation on all funds. You can disqualify an IRA account, for example, by using it as security for a loan, which is a prohibited transaction.[9] When this happens, your IRA account immediately becomes taxable, and its value is included in that year's tax return. It is therefore essential for the player to understand that what may seem to be innocent, lesser transgressions can sometimes result in horrific outcomes.

The Causes of Fouls and Penalties

In some games, such as golf, penalties are sometimes self-imposed. While it may seem surprising that anyone would self-penalize, there is a sound rationale behind this action. First, there are considerations of personal honesty and sportsmanship, which are of traditional importance in golf (in the 1925 US Open, legendary golfer Bobby Jones famously called a penalty on himself after accidentally moving his ball, even though no one had seen it happen).-

However, a more practical reason for a self-imposed penalty is that in some situations, the potential consequence of a foul called by the referee or by one's opponent is greater than the consequence of confessing to an error. For example, it may be better to refile an erroneous tax return than to have the IRS catch the error years later and mete out punishment. In other words, a small sin acknowledged is better than a great crime punished. In such a case, the taxpayer may be able to limit penalties and interest. Dragging one's feet in tax matters, especially when the player is aware that the fault is his, can exacerbate the repercussions when one is (inevitably) caught.

It would be a mistake, however, to think that all fouls and penalties are tax-driven. In fact, fouls and penalties can come from a number of sources; they can be market-driven, interest-driven, environment-driven, or systemic in nature.

Often players incur penalties out of ignorance. Altogether too many players don't acknowledge the rule book. In fact, many players don't even know that a rule book exists. Never assume that a rule is going to be provided for any given situation, or even that the pertinent rule is available as a coherent document. If there is any doubt, it is generally better for the player to investigate and find out whether an action violates a rule than to assume it doesn't. It can be prudent to assume you are in the wrong until you know otherwise.

Another complication of our game, one that even many skilled players fail to understand, is that there are multiple rule books in play for various games.[10] As a result, when a player goes astray, he can inadvertently break a number of rules in several different rule books in a single transaction. Obviously, when this happens, the consequences can undermine or cripple a player's game plan. Such is the effect of ignorance. It therefore benefits a player to ask himself whether he understands the basic, fundamental rules. For example, when does out-of-bounds occur? Are the boundaries breached when the player *touches* the white line (as in football or basketball)? Or are they breached when the white line is *crossed* (as in golf or baseball)? In other words, the simplest of matters—the definition of the field of play—can spell the difference between success and failure. This being the case, if the player feels that she does not properly understand the boundaries of the playing field, she would be well advised to seek guidance if it is available.[11]

The Environment, the Market, Interest Rates, and *the System*

In most cases, fouls and penalties can be avoided by simply understanding the rules and regulations. But since the definition of fouls and penalties can extend beyond what is obvious, let's explore other ways in which they can manifest themselves. As I mentioned earlier, there are causes of penalties and fouls other than tax issues. These include banking, market, environmental, or systemic issues. Environmental impacts are easy to understand, so let's explore them.

Some games aren't affected by weather; for example, college and professional basketball games normally are played in sterile, controlled environments. Other games, however, like baseball or golf, can be delayed or even cancelled because of weather. In yet other cases, games can be played under almost inhumane conditions: Football is played in the rain, in mud, and even in artic cold; soccer is played in extreme heat or in rain; and sailing often takes participants into extremely dangerous seas.

In the case of Wealth Transfer and Distribution, environment isn't often considered to have a practical effect . . . until one considers which way political winds are blowing.[12] As a settled example, consider how political winds changed the course of real estate investment for years with the passage of the Tax Reform Act of 1986.[13] The effect of this act was to overturn years of prior guidance and precedent, and to change how real estate could be depreciated and how its costs could be deducted. The impact of this change was significant enough to affect real estate as an asset class and as an investment for years to come. (Recall our discussions in previous chapters about Understanding the Rules and The Playing Field.)

The same kinds of serious change can occur with market and interest-rate risks. Because of the near-zero interest-rate environment of the past seven years, American retirees have been forced to change their investment behavior and adjust how they play the game if they want to preserve their capital. Since normal interest-bearing assets were effectively absent from the market (there have been virtual 0 percent yields on money market funds, less than inflation-rate interest paid on one-year CDs, and even circumstances in which banks required depositors to pay a fee for the bank to accept and hold deposits), people who otherwise lacked good reason or the means to accept risk were forced to modify their investment behavior in order to secure the cash flow they required to maintain their lifestyles.[14]

As we can see, environmental, interest-rate, and market risks can affect virtually everyone, from the poorest retiree to the wealthiest real estate magnate. Some might contend that these impacts are at the margins, but that attitude would be inaccurate. Systemic impacts are just as prevalent.[15]

Consider for a moment the effect of signature loans from 2007 to 2009. As a result of widespread loan-origination fraud, whether subsequently punished or not by governmental authorities, hundreds of thousands of homeowners were forced to abandon residential properties between 2008 and 2011. Easy money lending made entry painless but exit painful for borrowers who were neither initially qualified nor ultimately capable of absorbing rising interest-rate costs after the teaser-rate period. While this disaster has garnered much attention over the past few years, it is a clear indicator of what happens when the game is not played well: disaster for the player and his family! Obviously, in cases like these, the penalty for a game poorly played is not the downside of interest increases or underpayment penalties, as in income tax cases, but rather the loss of homes, personal bankruptcy, and ruined lives.[16] It should be clear that the failure to understand rules and regulations, and the impact of fouls and penalties, has ruined more than a few lives in the past ten years.

For this reason, it is essential that every potential player understand the potential negative consequences of his or her actions. Consequences need to be understood and made part of any reasonable strategic discussion. When these conversations don't occur, it becomes a matter of failed social policy affecting not only those who failed to anticipate the consequences of their actions, but also those who played the game wisely and responsibly. One of the less discussed results of the real estate bubble that burst earlier in this century was collateral damage—the impact of those foreclosed and repossessed homes on those who had played the game well. Players who understood how to play the game when it came to home purchases, who didn't overextend themselves, and who made their mortgage and property tax payments on time suffered alongside those who didn't when their home values were dragged down by their neighbors' foreclosures.[17]

This example illustrates that even when the game is well played by the individual, social mores can negatively affect results. It is not enough, then, to play the game well; it is necessary to make sure that others play the game equally well. Players who had observed the rules before and during the real estate bubble should have rained criticism and anger on the politicians who failed to uphold and support their proper behavior. Lawmakers neglected their responsibility to protect those who had abided by the rules. Unfortunately— and this is one of the inherent penalties in the game of Wealth Transfer and Distribution—it is not enough to win the game yourself. To truly win the game, the player must outwit and outplay *the system*, which is the least understood opponent.[18]

Finally, when it comes to fouls and penalties, it should be noted that one team has the power and authority to make changes in the rules. That team is the government, and to a lesser degree, its often-primary beneficiary, corporate America. Because one team has more power to effect rules changes than another, there can be little question of your personal interest in understanding how your efforts to play can be penalized.

Although we may not like them, there are good reasons for fouls and penalties. In a flawed system, fouls and their resulting penalties serve to level the playing field. As flawed as the game is, it is still worth playing. Fouls and penalties shouldn't discourage any player; after all, the game is on whether the player accepts that fact or not. Understanding how fouls are imposed and how penalties are assessed is one of the player's most important obligations, and a source of actual power. Avoiding the imposition of fouls and their consequent penalties should be every player's goal.

Notes

1. For an excellent and user-friendly guide to how the surviving spouse can decide what to do next, see Aviva Pinto, "On Your Own: Financial Advice After Losing a Spouse," *WealthManagement.com,* October 11, 2016. For those who think the prologue example is farfetched, see Donald A. Hamburg, "Discharge of Estate Tax Lien on Sale of Real Estate," *WealthManagement.com,* November 10, 2016. The IRS can surprise even experienced professional advisors with its interpretations and applications of the law.
2. Neeli Shah, "Intra-Family Loans: Real Debt or Gift," *Smith Gambrell and Russell, LLP,* October 11, 2011, and Julian Black, "How the IRS Tells a 'Loan' from a 'Gift,'" *Accounting Web,* May 12, 2014.
3. IRS Audit FAQs, *IRS.gov,* May 20, 2016.
4. "IRS Tax Fraud: Types and Penalties for Income Tax Fraud," *BackTaxesHelp.com,* 2015, and "Eight Facts on Late Filing and Late Payment Penalties," *IRS.gov,* May 18, 2013.
5. Even when we win, sometimes we lose; for a great example of how self-protection can go awry, see Steve Oshins, "In re Petition of Johnson: Decanting Gone Wrong," *Steve Leimberg's Estate Planning Newsletter,* March 16, 2015.
6. For detailed information on the innocent-spouse issue, see "Publication 971," *IRS.gov,* October 2014. This publication makes clear the challenges facing a spouse who claims ignorance.
7. Famous entertainers provide unfortunate yet excellent examples of what happens when things go wrong; see Juliette Farley, "The Downside of Sudden Wealth," *Private Wealth,* June 16, 2016.
8. Mark Dreschler, "Top 4 Mistakes Individual Trustees Make and How to Avoid Them," *Premier Trust,* May 2014.
9. For a quick introduction to the topic of prohibited transactions, see "Retirement Topics—Prohibited Transactions," *IRS.gov,* October 12, 2016.
10. Chuck Rubin, "US v. Spoor: Executor Loses Out on Fees Due to Section 6166 Lien," *Steve Leimberg's Estate Planning Newsletter,* November 17, 2016.
11. Complications arise when we expect help but can't get it. For a good example of how resources that should be available sometimes aren't, see Peter J. Johnson, "Corporate Fiduciaries Are Shying Away from Special Needs Trusts," *WealthManagement.com,* November 15, 2016.
12. "What Trump's Victory Means to You and Your Taxes," *MarketWatch,* November 12, 2016, and Ashlea Ebeling, "Will Trump Victory Yield Estate Tax Repeal?" *Forbes,* November 11, 2016.
13. Mark Mackenzie, "The Tax Reform Act of 1986 and Investment Real Estate," *activerain,* December 29, 2008.
14. Lauren Silva Laughlin, "Here's the Bad News about Long-Term Interest Rates," *Fortune,* April 5, 2016; and "Savings Hurt by Low Interest Rates? So Is Social Security, CBO Says," *The Senior Citizen League,* May 11, 2016.
15. Robert J. O'Regan, "Estate Plan Protects Widow from Son's Breach of Fiduciary Duty," *WealthManagement.com,* November 15, 2016.
16. Andrew Beattie, "Market Crashes: Housing Bubble & Credit Crisis," *Investopedia.* For a detailed study and analysis, see Todd J. Zywicki and Gabriel Okloski, "Working Paper: The Housing Market Crash," *Mercatus Center,* September 2009.

17. Alan L. Gustman, Thomas L. Steinmeier, and Nahid Tabatabai, "How Did the Recession of 2007–2009 Affect the Wealth and Retirement of Near Retirement Age Population in the Health and Retirement Study," *Social Security,* Volume 72, No. 4., 2012.

18. It becomes clear how difficult it can be to avoid penalties and consequent disappointment when we see how even the smartest and wealthiest can make mistakes and commit fouls. See Howard Zaritsky, "Webber v. Commissioner: Excessive Control Over Internal Investments Results in Taxation of Policy Owner on Income and Gains Inside Private Placement Variable Life Policy," *Steve Leimberg's Estate Planning Newsletter*, July 6, 2015.

Chapter 11

Distractions

———————◆———————

Prologue

The hallmark of our times is the sheer amount of information available. It's now possible to Google almost anything and get an answer immediately. However, getting information and having *quality* information are two different things. The problem with this proliferation of information is that much of it is just noise—partially true at best, and misinformation at worst.

Beyond the Internet, other distractions abound, often taking the form of friends and acquaintances who think they know a lot more than they actually do. These well-intentioned acquaintances are forever trying to do us the favor of sharing that "knowledge" with us. Unfortunately, the number of these people whose knowledge is actually supported by fact is hard to determine.

We are bombarded daily with advice from TV personalities, friends, relatives, and business associates, all of whom promise us the sun, moon, and stars if we heed their counsel. In my opinion, most of this noise is distracting, and in the game of Wealth Transfer and Distribution, distractions are dangerous.[1] Along these lines, one of the most common forms of distraction comes from "expert" financial advisors who operate in the gray areas of the rules and regulations.

Joe, a retired football player, fell prey to one of these service providers. Joe made a habit of listening to his friends and acquaintances, and because of his trusting nature, he assumed their opinions to be supported by fact. Like many other retired players (indeed, like most people his age), he spent a lot of time with old buddies, whether golfing, attending games, or just enjoying a cocktail. At one of these events, Joe met an "investment guru" who promised that he could realize fantastic returns from a proprietary investment idea.

This approach required Joe to invest a sizable amount of money upfront. In return, he was promised tax credits (dollar-for-dollar reductions in tax owed, as opposed to tax *deductions*, which lower the amount of taxable income before the tax is calculated). In addition to reduced taxes, Joe was promised a steady stream of tax-free income and was told that whatever gains he made would be both non-taxable and outside of his estate.[2] The advisor making this pitch urged Joe to move quickly, since he was enjoying a high-income year, working as a football broadcaster.

As far as Joe was concerned, this was the best of all possible worlds: He would reduce his taxes, receive tax-free cash flow, and tax-shelter this asset and its gains. It seemed too good to be true!

Not surprisingly, it *was* too good. Reality fell short of the promise; in place of tax credits, Joe got some deductions, but his tax savings were far less than he'd expected. He could have either tax-free income or a tax-sheltered asset and non-taxable gains, but not both. Joe had been sold a bill of goods. Unfortunately, I met Joe *after* he'd entered into this deal, and by then it was too late for him to get out.

After carefully reviewing the investment, we determined that the best thing Joe could do would be to understand his choices and act accordingly. Since the deal was already a couple of years old, the tax-credit issue was already exposed. Instead of a dollar-for-dollar tax credit, Joe used a portion of his contribution as deductions, thus lowering his taxable income. These deductions saved him less than forty cents on the dollar, however—considerably less than the substantial savings provided by tax credits.

The next step was to determine which of two options would be more valuable to him: getting a tax-free stream of income from an asset or exchanging that cash flow for an asset whose value would never be taxed. Joe chose the latter.

When everything was said and done, Joe concluded that his real benefits were significant, but far less than he'd been promised. Clearly, the advice he'd been given was incomplete and wrong, i.e., a distraction. What Joe learned was something he'd thought he already knew: If it seems too good to be true, it probably is! The good news was that this deal had some economic value. The bad news was that Joe could have employed more traditional investments and probably done equally well . . . and possibly better.

Distractions come in many forms, sometimes so cleverly cloaked in half-truths and promises as to seem legitimate. In this age of instant and seemingly all-inclusive information, we must be able to tell the difference between good and bad. Few people today still respond to promises of cash in e-mails originating from Nigeria—and yet, plenty of people still sign up for "free" credit cards, only to discover later that after the six-month introductory period, the interest rate on unpaid amounts exceeds 20 percent per year![3]

Distractions can creep into anyone's life. In the real estate lending debacle of 2006–2009, millions of homeowners found themselves trapped in loans that were interest-rate time bombs. After the inevitable explosions of these bombs, coupled with the decline of housing values in the same period, many people lost their homes to foreclosure. And many of those who didn't are still negatively affected ten years later.

It should be clear that caution is critical in the game of Wealth Transfer and Distribution. Failure to examine carefully what is advertised can carry a high cost. This is not to say that everything you read is wrong; it is to say, however, that you need to examine everything you read.

———— ♦ ————

Distractions are part of any game. They can take the form of trash-talking or the sound of a hundred thousand fans cheering for their team. The game of Wealth Transfer and Distribution has its own distractions, but these distractions are often subtler. The primary sources of distractions in our game are crowd noise, individual spectators, bright lights, and dark corners.

Crowd Noise

Crowd noise is probably the most obvious distraction in our game, and takes the form of what I call financial pornography. Financial pornography titillates with promises of easy money, instant success, excessive returns, or incredible tax savings. This form of crowd noise comes from half-truths in hyped-up media presentations, which seem to worsen yearly. Unfortunately, much of what we read and hear, especially about wealth transfer and distribution, is not true. At best, it is only partially true, and only under certain circumstances. Oftentimes what we read and hear from media sources represents opinions presented as fact, and failure to understand the difference is the reason why many players fail to reach their goals.

For example—and this should resonate with every player—Internet ads are notorious for misleading and often plainly wrong information. Broad, sweeping statements can be found on what are the best fifty stocks for next year, or how you should avoid annuities at all costs. Since there is no fact-checking service to confirm or debunk these claims, online sources should be read with skepticism.[4] In the game of Wealth Transfer and Distribution, player decisions must be predicated on what is *true*, as opposed to what is *believed*. Belief is not enough; decisions must be substantiated by evidence.

Being able to substantiate and defend a position makes for effective strategy and tactics. Given the complexity of the game's rules, it stands to reason that the player who can substantiate and defend her position is more likely to prevail than the player who relies on hearsay. Since the onus of proof is on the player, it is important to make sure that our positions are defensible. I am often amazed by clients who accept and promote positions based on wishful thinking. Wanting something to be true doesn't make it so.

In our game, being able to separate the signal from the noise is critical to success. I recommend that every player examine his or her position to make sure that it has basis in fact. Securing support for critical decisions from disinterested and capable third parties goes a long way toward backstopping our positions.[5] Attention to the most defensible positions can make all the difference in the world. For example, many times I have heard players state that the most they can give to each of their children in any one year is $10,000. Not only is this belief outdated (since the current exclusion amount is $14,000), but it is only a half-truth, since there are ways to make gifts of much greater amounts by using part of the player's lifetime allowance.

Every player must be able to justify what he or she believes and must make sure that belief is supported by fact. Learning to ignore grandiose statements is the usually the first step toward sound critical thinking.

Spectators

The second primary source of distraction comes from reliance on what the player hears from friends. When friends and acquaintances represent their opinions as fact, two players are adversely affected: the person promulgating the incorrect information and the player who accepts this information as fact. Cocktail talk, golf course chatter, and coffeehouse discussion needs to be vetted with care. I fully appreciate the good intentions of friends sharing opinions, but the harm caused by these casual conversations can be considerable. Clearly there are ideas that come from these discussions that merit consideration, but in my opinion, substantiation by a coach or specialist is necessary. Every player can improve his game by cultivating a coaching staff that knows his goals and objectives and can evaluate new ideas in light of what the player is trying to accomplish.[6]

When it comes to individual spectators, it is often difficult to tamp down someone else's enthusiasm. The best thing to do is to make sure that the latest great idea works for *you*. For example, as we discussed in chapter 4, in recent years it has been possible for taxpayers older than 70½ to make gifts to charity directly from their IRA accounts in a streamlined tax process. While this is an attractive approach for many wealthy people, it is available only to taxpayers who meet the age requirement; for players under the age of 70½, this strategy results in a different, more complicated tax result. In both cases, the gift can be made, but being the right age makes all the difference if the goal is a streamlined transaction. If a sixty-five-year-old player learns about this option, he may assume incorrectly that he and his older friend will enjoy the same tax treatment. Unfortunately, he would be mistaken. The word of a good friend doesn't make something good or right. This source of distraction should be watched carefully.

Bright Lights

Bright lights are another source of distraction in our game. Most games are played under bright lights for a reason: to ensure that everyone can see what is happening and, hopefully, minimize challenges and protests. The Wealth Transfer and Distribution game is often played under bright lights because the techniques involved are subject to legal and tax challenges, which tend to peel away outside layers until the core of the activity is laid open. As a result, bright lights are sometimes a distraction because they can discourage a player from subjecting herself to public scrutiny and make her unwilling to play the game at all. Arguably, this is the cost of transparency.[7]

For many players, especially those who push their positions to the margins of what can be defended, bright lights serve as a different form of distraction. In these cases, at least in terms of social policy, the distraction is a positive one for society at large. Transparency and clarity are desirable in the game of Wealth Transfer and Distribution. Having players who seek to shade part of the field *isn't* desirable. Throughout history, players have tried to take permitted activities and stretch their boundaries and uses to accommodate objectives that were never intended to be allowed. In these cases, players try to bend the rules to get an additional or increased benefit.

There are many examples of this behavior; one of the easiest to understand is what happens when some players use life insurance to protect themselves from the loss of key employees in a company. It makes complete sense for a corporation to insure the life of a key executive; losing the services of an employee who contributes substantially to a corporation's ability to compete is a real risk. Take Steve Jobs for example: During his tenure at Apple, his ingenuity and creativity made Apple a far more profitable enterprise than it would have been without him. Clearly, Jobs had economic value to Apple, and it would have made economic sense for Apple to insure itself against the loss of his life and services (hypothetically speaking; I'm not aware of them actually having done so). This kind of insurance is called "key-person coverage" and it is perfectly justifiable.

Other companies, however, decided to expand on this idea, and took it to an illogical extreme; they insured virtually all of their employees, right down to the janitors. This attracted the attention of the IRS, for an obvious reason: tax-free insurance payouts received by these corporations upon the deaths of these employees. While it would have been valid for Apple to insure against the loss of Steve Jobs, there are no grounds for another company to insure against the loss of a janitor. Tax authorities ultimately ruled against allowing these same kinds of tax benefits to companies that insured any and all employees. In this case, the bright light of legal scrutiny closed down a position that lacked validity.[8]

How do these bright lights become a potential distraction in our game? Simply, they may intimidate our player and cause him to avoid playing the game. In this way, they constitute a distraction. It is critical to note, however, that bright lights are a problem only if you fail to observe the rules and regulations. I have seen many players shy away from respected, valid strategies and tactics for fear of the scrutiny of bright lights. In so doing, they deprived themselves of potential benefits. This is where managers, coaches, and specialists can come together and make the argument that there is nothing to fear from bright lights if you are playing the game as it should be played. Fearing bright lights for their own sake can cripple a player's willingness to play the game, and the effect of this kind of fear can be profound.

Finally, sometimes a new idea is worth the risk of attracting the bright lights. Challenging the rules is justified when circumstances suggest that you have a valid case to make. Since the rules and regulations change regularly, it is frequently necessary for players to determine where the new boundaries lie. Stepping forward with a new idea or approach, while intimidating and costly, may sometimes be the best and right thing to do.[9] For example, one of my clients, Walter, once took a position that even most of his specialists and coaches questioned. He claimed that he was a real estate professional, despite the fact that he owned a consulting business that demanded a fair amount of his time. Because of this business, the IRS initially denied him the benefits they normally accord to real estate professionals. By supplying records and receipts, however, Walter demonstrated beyond a doubt that his primary occupation was managing and improving his real estate holdings . . . and he prevailed. Because his supporting information and documentation were so strong, he ultimately accomplished more than even he anticipated. Not a bad result for an argument that his advisors initially viewed as having little chance for success.

Bright lights, therefore, are not all bad. It is distracting and scary to be in the spotlight, but by being prepared and supported, a good player can make his time under the bright lights beneficial.

The first night game in the history of Major League Baseball was played on May 24, 1935, between the Cincinnati Reds and the Philadelphia Phillies at Crosley Field in Cincinnati. Ever since that evening over eighty years ago, ballplayers have had to contend with bright lights on an almost nightly basis. The glare of massive, powerful floodlights and the intense scrutiny of fifty thousand spectators never threw David Ortiz off his game, and it shouldn't throw you off yours.

Dark Corners

Dark corners are our last distraction. Even in the brightest light, there are dark corners. Dark corners are understood best as circumstances that can trap us or deceive us. For example, despite a benign appearance, the ivy-covered walls at Wrigley Field have always been a dark corner. Every once in a while, a ball hit to the outfield gets lost in the ivy. Despite the outfielder's best efforts, the ball can't be found. The same kind of event can happen in golf, when a ball hit to the center of a sloping fairway can't be found because the pitch of the fairway is so severe as to have pulled it into heavy rough or a parallel water hazard. In both these cases, these unexpected dark corners create problems.

The same is true in the game of Wealth Transfer and Distribution: Strange things can and do happen. For example, one wouldn't think that an insurance policy owned by Mom, insuring Dad, and payable to the children will create an income tax issue, but it will.[10] Similarly, owning a special type of investment in an IRA account can create a form of income that can disqualify the entire IRA account and result in immediate income taxation on the entire balance. Very few players ever hear the term "Unrelated Business Taxable Income" (UBTI),[11] but its presence in an IRA account can be deadly. Simply said, unexpected issues arising from seemingly benign circumstances bring us face to face with dark corners that yield unexpected and unwelcome results.

The point here is that a player should never assume the best. It is essential for the player to know the environmental hazards (which way the fairway slopes and whether there is a lake waiting for his ball) and to take the necessary precautions to avoid them. This may be as simple as asking, "Is there anything that I should know about what I am about to do that I am unlikely to have considered?" This amounts to testing the course, the hole, and the shot *before* it is played—as there are, in many cases, no opportunities to remedy our mistakes once we have taken our initial actions.

———— ♦ ————

In the game of Wealth Transfer and Distribution, the best players do the following in order to minimize distractions:

◊ They examine what they hear or read, and carefully consider whether what is presented actually conforms to the advice of their coaches and specialists.

◊ They listen to friends' and acquaintances' opinions, but evaluate them carefully, considering whether there is satisfactory substance behind the idea, and allowing for the possibility that the other player's goals may differ.

◊ They get used to bright lights and don't shy away from the playing field just because all eyes are on them; if what they believe has substance, they welcome the bright lights as a means of justifying their positions.

◊ They avoid dark corners when they can, but when those corners cannot be avoided, they take the time to determine whether they have options that can lessen the potential penalties they face.

Distractions are found everywhere in life, so it shouldn't be surprising that they appear in the game of Wealth Transfer and Distribution. These distractions must be managed in order to ensure that they don't become the focus of the player's activity. And whenever possible, distractions should be used to the player's advantage.

Notes

1. One of the better recent discussions on the proliferation of information is a wonderful book by Nate Silver, titled *The Signal and the Noise: Why So Many Predictions Fail—but Some Don't*. Reading this book will help almost anyone understand the danger of too much unfiltered information and the risk of drawing the wrong conclusions from the information we have on hand. In our game, separating the signal from the noise is very important because our accomplishments can be diluted by the wrong conclusions.

2. For an introduction to abusive retirement plans, see "EP Abusive Tax Transactions," *IRS. gov,* May 12, 2016, and "Treasury & IRS Shut Down Abusive Life Insurance Policies in Retirement Plans," *IRS.gov,* August 18, 2012.

3. "Credit Card Teaser Rates," *Investopedia*: http://www.investopedia.com/terms/c/credit-card-teaser-rate.asp.

4. After the 2016 Presidential election, particular attention has been given to "fake news" sites purporting to be reliable news sources. For more detail, see Joe Mandes, "Facebookers 2.5 Times More Likely to Read Fake News, Millennials Least Prone," *Publishers Daily,* November 25, 2016.

5. For a dispassionate overview of a complicated subject, see Brian Jacobsen and James Kochan, "An Insider's Guide to Bond Opportunities," *Wells Fargo,* August 2016. In my experience, most investors have a more difficult time understanding how bonds work than they do understanding stocks. A guide that presents this subject clearly and dispassionately can be useful. Also see Rich Dunn, "8 Signs Your Estate Plan Is Off Track," *Farm Futures,* October 25, 2016.

6. If you need further convincing on this matter, please review chapter 5 on building your team.

7. Suzanne Wooley, "You Don't Want to Be on the Radar of the IRS Wealth Squad," *Accounting Today,* September 26, 2016. For a good example of what happens when you find yourself at odds with the IRS, see Jay Adkisson, "US v. Baker: US District Court Finds Divorce Obtained to Fraudulently Transfer Assets," *Steve Leimberg's Asset Protection Planning Newsletter,* September 10, 2015.

8. Theo Francis and Ellen E. Schultz, "Case Shows How 'Janitors Insurance' Works to Boost Employers' Earnings," *WSJ.online,* April 25, 2002, and David McCann, "'Dead Peasant Insurance' Still Alive in Corporate America," *CFO,* January 31, 2014. This practice, which many people find ghoulish and which was considered once dead, seems still to have its proponents.

9. America seems fascinated by superheroes; every year several movies come out featuring familiar heroes (e.g., Superman, Batman) or heroes new to many of us (e.g., Doctor Strange). In the world of "bright lights," we also can find superheroes—professionals who find value in advocating tax positions that stretch the law to its logical ends. One of these superheroes is Texas attorney John W. Porter, who has positively affected many tax court cases. I suggest Googling him to see the success he has enjoyed. You will be impressed!

10. "Avoiding the Goodman Rule," *MetLife Investors,* 2014.

11. UBIT and UBTI are little understood because of their arcane nature. Certain investments create Unrelated Business Taxable Income (UBTI), which in turn creates Unrelated Business Income Tax (UBIT). For a primer on UBTI and UBIT, see "What is UBIT?" *NewDirectionIRA.com*, and "Self-Directed IRA Rules and Regulations: UBIT," *Equity Trust.*

Chapter 12

Conclusion

———————◆———————

By now, I hope that you realize that regardless of whether you have a modest home to transfer to your children or an estate worth billions, you are playing a game. Your ability to master this game depends upon your ability to identify, understand, and master the opportunities this game affords you. The better you prepare, the more you know, and the better the team you gather, the greater the chances you will succeed at this game and leave it a winner. By contrast, walking into this game unprepared could have dire consequences for you and those you love. It is quite possible to wrest defeat from the jaws of victory. Equally important, this is a game that you can and likely will play once or hundreds of times, with each actual game defined by its individual goals and objectives.

It is not necessary or even likely that you will ever play the same game twice. Changes occur from game to game, which will require modifications in strategies or tactics. These changes can be the result of legal, tax, market, personal, or environmental factors. In the end, your success at the game of Wealth Transfer and Distribution is dependent upon your willingness to put together the team you need and allow them to help you win the game. You can decide to wear every hat in the games you play, but my experience suggests that this approach is not likely to deliver the best results, and that the downside of playing without managers, coaches, and specialists becomes more significant the more complicated your goals and objectives become.

Like all games, the game of Wealth Transfer and Distribution can be replayed years after the actual play date. In other words, not only can you revisit the game, but in some situations, the final outcome may not be apparent until after the end of your life. For example, a dear friend and client of mine is benefitting today from a trust formed in the 1930s and ultimately will be distributed upon his death, which could be another fifteen to twenty years in the future. All things considered, few things are more satisfying than reliving a game well played; whether it is basking in the afterglow of a tennis club championship or reliving the glory days of your favorite football team, remembrance is a vital part of any game. Success in the game of Wealth Transfer and Distribution is no different; tangible success delivers satisfaction.

Over the last thirty-plus years, I have helped families design plans that deliver the benefits of business succession or wealth transfer to third and even fourth generations—during a time and in an environment in which few family businesses survive two generations of ownership. I have seen grandchildren follow their dreams and deliver socially beneficial results because earlier generations had believed in their grandchildren educating impoverished children. Playing the game of Wealth Transfer and Distribution well affords choices to families. It is not only money that is distributed, but family values as well.

At the same time, when the game of Wealth Transfer and Distribution has been ignored or badly played, I have seen families waste time, effort, money, and family relationships, essentially ruining their prospects for happiness. Businesses failed, properties languished, and discord drove subsequent generations apart, all because the game of Wealth Transfer and Distribution was either played poorly or ignored.

Several years ago I met a puzzling man who, despite his success and intelligence, refused to address the game-playing issues facing him. In fact, he went so far as to tell me that he planned never to die. When he *did* die two years later, he left his family affairs in such shambles that by the time his estate was settled, family unity had been destroyed, properties needed to be leveraged, siblings had become enemies, and everything he and his family had worked so hard to build since they'd come to America after the Holocaust was teetering on the brink of failure. Happily, the family fortune wasn't lost in the end; it *was* badly depleted, however, and the survivors were unable to work together. As a result, not only were assets affected, but family ties were also so badly damaged that a mother and her child never spoke again.

I hope I have convinced you that wealth transfer and distribution is not something that just happens. When I first started advising wealthy families, I penned a statement for clients to consider: "The future doesn't just happen; it must be planned." Little did I know then that this would become the basis for my professional efforts over the following decades. I know this: If you have almost anything of worth, you will be exposed to the game of Wealth Transfer and Distribution whether you actively and purposely participate or not. My challenge to you is to play well; if you don't play the game, the game will play you.

Over the next twenty to thirty years, $16–$60 trillion in assets will be in play in the United States. While I haven't made dollars or value the focus of my discussion, be clear on this one point: This will be the single largest wealth transfer in history. How this transfer and distribution plays out is going to carry social and political ramifications, in addition to the obvious economic impacts. What happens to America in the next fifty years is likely to have roots in this transfer. Today there is much discussion about the erosion and disappearance of the middle class. I am not prepared to say that the fate of the middle class hinges on this wealth transfer and distribution (although that may be the case). I do believe that the health and well-being of many individual families will be affected by what happens.

Through my efforts there are two hundred client families whose futures ride on how they play this game. It comforts me to know that because these two hundred owners and players are making good use of managers, coaches, and specialists, they stand a far better chance of successfully delivering assets to their children and grandchildren than many other players. I believe that these families will be able to reminiscence thirty years from now on the efforts of their parents and grandparents, who chose to play the game of Wealth Transfer and Distribution to the best of their abilities.

End Note Addendum

A characteristic of Playing the Game is the dynamic nature of information, design, concerns, and ideas. If there is one truism about planning Wealth Transfer and Distribution, it is that change is constant. For this reason, despite having completed the text of this book in December 2016, I believed that it would be a disservice to you as a reader to provide anything other than the most up-to-date information.

For this reason, I include this addendum dedicated to the highest quality topical information from January 1 to June 30, 2017. The cut-off date is due to the limitations of publication. Morgan James needs to have adequate time to create the final product without change. As a generous concession to us, Morgan James allowed me the opportunity to add information from the first six months of 2017.

Unlike the Chapter End Notes in the text, these End Notes are arranged by chapter in chronological order. In almost every instance the title defines the material discussed. In those few instances where there is confusion, I added a brief comment for context. In those instances where several articles belong together, I added them to the first article. Hopefully, this approach assists in satisfying your interest.

Additional End Notes

CHAPTER 1 – Introduction to the Game
No additional material

CHAPTER 2 – Defining the Game

1. Scott Martin, 'Carrie Fisher and Debbie Reynolds Dynastic Deaths Give Offspring Legacies and Millions to Inherit Overnight,' *WealthAdvisor*, January 2, 2017.
2. Steve Vernon, 'The Problem with This Boomer "Retirement Plan",' *CBS Moneywatch*, January 3, 2017. Also, Karen Demasters, 'Advisors Help People Ease Stress Over Retirement Income,' *Financial Advisor*, January 10, 2017; Luke Kawa, 'Older Americans Are Retiring in Droves,' *Financial Advisor* January 13, 2017; Amy Florian, 'Twelve Steps to Ease Clients into a Happier Retirement,' Wealthmanagement.com, February 28, 2017; 'The 18 Risks of Retirement Income Planning,' *The American College of Financial Services*, March 2017; and John Mauldin, 'Angst In America, Part 6: Middle Class Blues,' *Thoughts from the Frontline*, April 30, 2017.
3. John Manganaro, 'Young Investors Fuel Advice Market Growth,' *Planadviser*, January 4, 2017. Also, Matt Matrisian, 'Strategies For Reaching Millennial Investors,' *Wealthmanagement.com*, March 15, 2017; John Mauldin, 'Angst in America, Part 7: The Angst of the Millennial Generation,' *Thoughts from the Frontline*, May 7, 2017; Gary D. Halbert, 'Over One-Third of Millennials Live with Their Parents,' *Forecast & Trends*, June 27, 2017; and John Hawthorne, 'Six Ways Millennials Are Changing Charitable Giving,' *Wealthmanagement.com*, June 27, 2017.
4. Martin M. Shenkman, Andrew T. Wolfe, and Alan A. Davidson, 'Repeal and Uncertainty Impacts Estate Administration,' *Wealthmanagement.com*, January 5, 2017. Also, 'Do You Still Need an Estate Plan if There Isn't an Estate Tax?' Forbes, March 24, 2017; Charlie Douglas, '"Estate Planning" Needs an Extreme Makeover,' *Wealthmanagement.com*. May 15, 2017; and Patrick Carlson, 'DINKs Need Estate Planning Too,' *Wealthmanagement.com*, May 30, 2017.

5.   Ed McCarthy, 'Financial Wellness Programs Will Thrive in 2017,' *Wealthmanagement.com*, January 12, 2017.

6.   Barbara Marquand, 'How To Prepare Financially for Your Death (No Matter How Young You Are),' *USA Today*, January 16, 2017. Also, Dr. David Eifrig, 'How to Prepare Your Spouse for the Worst-Case Scenario,' The Crux, January 24, 2017 and David H. Lenok, 'Seven Tips for Protecting Clients from Elder Abuse,' *Wealthmanagement.com*, June 9, 2017.

7.   Russ Alan Prince, 'Estate Planning for the Ultra-Wealthy When Living to 120 or Beyond,' *Forbes*, January 18, 2017. Also, Victor Nagal, 'Six Longevity Tips to Discuss with Clients,' *Wealthmanagement.com*, April 19, 2017; 'The Rich Are Living Longer and Taking More from Taxpayers,' *Wealth Advisor*, April 24, 2017; and John Mauldin, "Can You Afford to Reach 100?' Thoughts from the Frontline, June 3, 2017.

8.   Robert Keebler and Steve Oshins, '10 Best Estate Planning Strategies for 2017,' *Wealthmanagement.com*, January 19, 2017.

9.   John Kador, 'The Index: The Great Wealth Transfer.' *Wealthmanagement.com*, January 27, 2017. Also, David H. Lenok, 'Americans Aren't Ready for the Great Wealth Transfer,' *Wealthmanagement.com*, February 1, 2017; Will Sleeth, 'Top Estate Disputes of 2016,' *Wealthmanagement.com*, January 31, 2017; Michael Thrasher, 'Wide Gaps in Financial Literacy Transcend Generations, Study Finds,' *Wealthmanagement.com*, April 5, 2017; and 'Clueless About Retirement: Americans Fail Retirement Income Quiz,' The American College of Financial Services, May 2017.

10.   Mark Eghrari, 'When You Pass Away, Don't Just Leave Assets to Your Heirs. Leave Memories,' *Forbes*, January 30, 2017. Also, Mark Eghrari, 'Where Inheritance Is Concerned, Equal May Not Be Fair,' *Forbes*, February 27, 2017 and Shari Burns, 'Key Considerations for Preparing a Family Legacy Plan, *Wealthmanagement.com*, March 27, 2017.

11.   Janice A. Forgays, 'Overlooked or Underappreciated Reasons for Estate Planning,' *Trusts & Estates*, February 2017, pages 81-86.

12.   Herbert R. Fineberg, 'Inheritance Planning Using Bloodline Multi-Generational Trusts,' *The Legal Intelligencer*, February 14, 2017.

13.   Gil Weinrich, 'Even the Rich Can't Afford Retirement,' Seeking Alpha, March 23, 2017.

14.   Kevin McKinley, 'Six Financial Planning Steps for Expecting Parents,' *Wealthmanagement.com*, March 31, 2017.

15.   Bruce Wolfe and Russ Koesterich, 'Demographics Are Destiny,' *Seeking Alpha*, April 4, 2017.

16.   Blanche Lark Christerson, 'Saving For College,' *Tax Topics*, May 31, 2017.

17.   For a thoughtful guide to the kind of attributes your estate planning attorney should bring to the table, see L. Paul Hood, 'Thirty-Two Core Beliefs,' *Trusts & Estates*, April 2017.

18.   Eloise Stiglitz, 'An Advisor's Guide to Aging in Place vs. Community Living,' *Wealthmanagement.com*, June 29, 2017.

CHAPTER 3 – Understanding the Rules

1.   Jason Harrel, 'Estate Planning Under a Trump Administration,' *Central Valley Business Journal*, January 18, 2017. Also, David H. Lenok, 'Life after Death Tax,' *Wealthmanagement.com*, January *Wealthmanagement.com*23, 2017; John Mauldin, 'Tax Reform: The Good, the Bad, and the Ugly – Part One,' *Thoughts from the Frontline*, February 7, 2017; Blanche Lark Christerson, 'On the Way to Tax Reform,' Tax Topics, February 28, 2017; Kevin Matz, 'Trump's Tax Plan Raises Questions for Estate Planners,'

Wealthmanagement.com, April 28, 2017; and The Hill, 'As Congress Debates Repeal of the Estate Tax, Why Not Consider Ending the Gift Tax?, *Wealth Advisor*, June 22, 2017.

2.   Mark Miller, 'States' Rights? Not So Much When It Comes to Retirement Savings,' *Wealthmanagement.com*, February 16, 2017. Also, Darla Mercado, 'House Votes to Block Rule Expanding Sate-Run IRA Programs,' CNBC, February 15, 2017 and David Armstrong, 'Will GOP Tax Plan 401(k) Savers,' *Wealthmanagement.com*, March 20, 2017.

3.   For a current discussion on the issue of form over substance, see Peter Melcher & Grant Keebler, 'Summa Holdings v. Commissioner,' *Steve Leimberg's Employee Benefits and Retirement Planning Newsletter*, March 17, 2017 and Ben Steveman, 'Republicans Take Aim at California's Retirement Dream,' *Wealthmanagement.com*, March 29, 2017.

4.   Alison E. Lothes and David A. Handler, 'IRS Changes Estate Lien Process,' *Wealthmanagement.com*, April 17, 2017. Also, Phyllis Horn Epstein, "Private Debt Collection Arrives at the IRS,' *Steve Leimberg's Income Tax Planning Newsletter*, April 4, 2017.

5.   For a comprehensive overview of the proposed Trump tax plan, see Robert S. Keebler, 'Trump Tax Plan,' *Leimberg Information Services*, May 1, 2017. Also, Sandra G. Swinski, 'White House Takes Over Reins of Tax Reform,' Wealthmanagment.com, May 1, 2017.

6.   Owen Fiore, 'Estate of Powell: Tax Court Again Rejects Deathbed Use of the Value-Discounting FLP to Reduce Estate Tax,' *Steve Leimberg's Estate Planning Email Newsletter*, June 1, 2017.

7.   'IRS Offers Estate Tax Relief to Widows and Widowers,' *Forbes*, June 12, 2017.

8.   Michael Thrasher, 'Other States Consider Their Own 'Fiduciary Rules' After Nevada's Become Law,' *Wealthmanagement.com*, June 26, 2017.

CHAPTER 4 – The Playing Field

1.   Francesco Florenzano and Giulio Allevato, 'Italy: New Beneficial Tax Regime for New Residents,' *Wealthmanagement.com*, January 4, 2017. Also, Mark Buchanan, 'Tax Havens Can Be Surprisingly Close to Home,' *Wealthmanagement.com*, April 11, 2017.

2.   Andrew Osterland, 'Estate-Planning Pros Take Wait-and-See Approach to Trump,' CNBC, January 11, 2017. Also, Kevin Matz, 'Reimagining Estate Planning in 2017,' *Wealthmanagement.com*, February 10, 2017; Ben Lee, 'Repeal of Estate Tax Under Trump Could Lead to More Confusion for Planners,' *Wealth Advisor*, February 21, 2017; and Michael J. Nathanson, Ian D. Barclay, and Cary P. Geller, 'Estate Planning: It's Not Over,' Financial Advisor, April 25, 2017.

3.   Danielle Sabrina, "DOL's New Fiduciary Ruling Pushing Financial Advisors to Seek Better Technology,' *Huffpost*, February 22, 2017.

4.   Jed Davis, 'Cybersecurity for Family Offices,' *Wealthmanagement.com*, February 24, 2017. Also, 'Seven Ways to Keep Your Financial Information Secure Online,' *Forbes*, March 21, 2017.

5.   'Majority of Wealthy Investors Prefer a Mix of Human and Robo-Advice, According to Accenture Research,' BusinessWire, March 30, 2017. Also, Ed McCarthy, 'Robo Services Focus on Plan Marketplace,' *Wealthmanagement.com*, April 25, 2017; Nick Murray, 'Wake Up to the Golden Age of Financial Planning,' Financial Advisor, May 16, 2017; Ryan W. Neal, 'Could a Robo Advisor Know a Client As Well As a Human?' *Wealthmanagement. com*, June 8, 2017; and Scott Martin, 'The Future of the Advisor Is ... Everywhere,' *Wealth Advisor*, June 15, 2017.

6.   Steve Oshins, '8th Annual Domestic Asset Protection Trust State Rankings,' *Steve Leimberg's Asset Protection Planning Newsletter*, April 24, 2017. Also, Gino Pascucci, 'How Nevada Became America's Safest State for Wealth Protection,' *Wealth Advisor*, June 29, 2017.

7. Scott Mined, 'The Keys to American Growth,' *Advisor Perspectives*, May 5, 2107. Also, Alexander Green, '20 Reasons Why America Is Still the Greatest Nation,' *The Crux*, May 30, 2017.

8. Bruce Steiner, 'Matter of Blatt: Home IS Where Your Dog Is,' *Steve Leimberg's Income Tax Planning Newsletter*, June 17, 2017.

CHAPTER 5 – Building Your Team

1. Diane Bell, 'Six Things Family-Owned Firms Should Know About Succession Planning,' *Wealthmanagement.com*, January 12, 2017. Also, David H. Lenok, 'What Siblings Fight About and How Advisors Can Help,' *Wealthmanagement.com*, June 21, 2017.

2. Larry Greenberg, 'What Investors Want from Their Advisor,' *Financial Advisor*, January 16, 2017. Also, Karen Demasters, '10 Ways FAs Resolve to Make Practices Better in New Year,' *Financial Advisor*, January 17, 2017; Matt Oechsli, 'Is Your Inner Circle Holding You Back?' *Wealthmanagement.com*, January 19, 2017; Kevin Meehan, 'The *Financial Advisor* As Life Coach,' *Wealthmanagement.com*, February 10, 2017; Erik Christman, 'Advice for Choosing a Financial Advisor You Can Trust,' *Forbes*, February 16, 2017; 'Do Your Clients Understand What You're Saying?' Advisor Perspectives, February 21, 2017; Gil Weinrich, 'Why Investors Are Often Frustrated by Their Advisors,' *Financial Advisors' Daily Digest*, February 23, 2017; Matt Oechsli, 'Emotionally Connecting With Clients,' *Wealthmanagement.com*, March 2, 2017; Bob Curtis, 'Why Financial Advisors Need to Be Coaches,' *Financial Advisor,* April 10. 2017; and 'Are You the Financial Advisor Clients Trust?' CNBC, June 24, 2017.

3. Mark Miller, 'Younger Americans Embrace the Value of Unbiased Financial Advice,' *Reuters*, January 18, 2017. Also, Michael Thrasher, 'Half of Affluent Millennials Are Planning to Switch Advisory Firms: J.D. Power Survey,' *Wealthmanagement.com*, April 6, 2017; David H. Lenok, 'HNW Millennials Are Hungry for Advice … from Humans,' *Wealthmanagement.com*, April 13, 2017; and Seth R. Kaplan, 'Counseling Gen X Clients,' *Wealthmanagement.com*, June 19, 2017.

4. Elizabeth Harris, 'The Last Taboo: Your Parents Still Won't Talk About Money,' *Forbes*, January 31, 2017. Also, Karen Demasters, 'Who Holds the Purse Strings for Couples?' Financial Advisor, April 7, 2017; Jared Dillian, 'Are You Good With Money?' The 10th Man, April 13, 2017; Matt Oechsli, 'The ABC Delegation System.' *Wealthmanagement. com*, May 3, 2017; Mark Palmerino, 'How Best to Support Politically Divided Couples,' *Wealthmanagement.com*, May 8, 2017; Anna Sulkin, 'Withholding Inheritance Details – More Harm than Good,' *Wealthmanagement.com*, May 10, 2017; and Beverly Flaxington, 'Whether to Counsel Clients on Spending Habits,' *Advisor Perspectives*, May 22, 2017 .

5. 'Are Wealth Management Firm Owners Missing an Opportunity?' *Wealth Advisor*, January 31, 2017. Also, Steven Dudash, 'Three Ways Independent Advisors Need to Adapt to Truly Be 'Full Service',' *Wealthmanagement.com*, February 14, 2017 and Deborah Nason, 'More Advisors Adding 'Financial Counseling' to Services Menu,' CNBC, April 3, 2017.

6. Megan Leonhardt, 'Everything You Need to Know about Using and Choosing a Robo-Advisor,' *Money*, January 17, 2017. Also, Robert Powell, 'Can Investors Trust a Robot to Work in Their Best Interest?' MarketWatch, March 22, 2017.

7. Paul Katzeff, 'Make Love, Not War? How Financial Advisors Decide When to Collaborate,' *Investor's Business Daily*, February 24, 2017. Also, Martin M. Shenkman, Collaboration,' Shenkman *Practical Planner*, January-March 2017 and Brian O'Connell, 'Financial Advisors Shouldn't Double as Portfolio Managers,' *TheStreet*, April 11, 2017.

8. Kathleen Burns Kingsbury, 'What Female Investors Want from Their Advisors,' *Advisor Perspectives*, March 28, 2017.

9. Ryan W. Neal, 'Bringing Advice to Underserved Communities,' *Wealthmanagement.com*, April 5, 2017.
10. Phyllis Horn Epstein, 'Help around the House & What It Could Cost You,' *Steve Leimberg's Income Tax Planning Newsletter*, April 26, 2017. Also, Barry A. Nelson & Cassandra Nelson, 'Attorneys Face Difficult Ethical Challenges in Trying to Protect Clients from Financial Elder Abuse/Exploitation,' *Steve Leimberg's Elder Care Law Planning Newsletter*, June 5, 2017.

CHAPTER 6 – Keeping Score

1. Gary Halbert, 'Most Americans Retire Too Soon Despite Low Savings,' *Forecasts & Trends*, January 3, 2017. Also, Ben Steverman, 'Americans Are Saving Billions More than Usual in the 401(k)s,' *Financial Advisor*, January 4, 2017; Russ Hill and Sam Pittman, ' Rethinking Retirement Liability,' *Financial Advisor*, February 15, 2017; Lance Roberts, 'The Fatal Flaws in Your Financial Plan,' Advisor Perspectives, February 21, 2017; Ben Steverman,' 'Two-Thirds of Americans Aren't Putting Money in their 401(k),' *Financial Advisor*, February 21, 2017; George Schneider, 'You've Accumulated $1 Million: What Do You Value Most: Cash Flow or Capital Appreciation?' *Seeking Alpha*, February 25, 2017; Suzanne Woolley, 'More Americans Live in Fear of Retiring Poor,' Bloomberg, February 28, 2017; David Blanchett, Michael S. Finke, and Wade D. Pfau, 'Planning for a More Expensive Retirement,' *Journal of Financial Planning*, March 2017; Mark Miller, 'The Rising Cost of $1 in Retirement Income,' *Wealthmanagement.com*, March 24, 2017; John Mauldin, 'Angst In America, Part 3: Retiring Broke,' *Thoughts from the Frontline*, April3, 2017; 'Retirement Strategy: Will You Crash Into the Retirement Crisis Ahead?' *Seeking Alpha*, April 19. 2017; and Katherine Chiglinsky, 'Retirement Savings Gap Seen Reaching $400 Trillion by 2050,' *Financial Advisor*, May 26, 2017
2. Michael Gilfix, 'How Trump Policies Could Affect the Elderly and Those with Special Needs,' *Wealthmanagement.com* January 6, 2017. Also, Marvin Blum, 'When Clients Need to See Red,' *Wealthmanagement.com*, February 8, 2017; 'Are You Testing Older Clients' Portfolios,' WealthAdvisor, April 14, 2017; and Suzanne Woolley, 'How Much to Save for Health Care in Retirement,' *Wealthmanagement.com*, June 22, 2017
3. Elizabeth Harris, 'Quiz: What's Your Financial Confidence? (Hint: It Has Nothing to Do with Income),' *Forbes*, January 10, 2017. Also, 'Know How to Act When You Feel like You're about to React,' *Nationwide*, January 20, 2017; Gil Weinrich, 'How to Add (or Subtract) Zeroes to Your Retirement Income,' *Seeking Alpha*, February 14, 2017; David Easter, 'Have Confidence that You Can Retire Without Changing Your Lifestyle: Here's How,' *Seeking Alpha*, February 22, 2017; Robert Laura, 'The Most Frightening Yet Most Important Rule that Baby Boomers Still Need to Break,' *Forbes*, February 27, 2017; George Schneider, 'Baby Steps to Giants Steps: Retirement, One Dividend At a Time,' *Seeking Alpha*, April 11, 2017; and 'Personal Retirement Paycheck: Tips to Help Clients Retire Smart,' *Wealthmanagement.com*, May 30, 2017
4. 'Millennials ARE Worse off than Their Parents,' *DailyMail.com*, January 19, 2017. Also, "Why Millennials Aren't Happy About Their Financial Prospects,' Attn, January 15, 2017 and John Kador, 'Eight Charts That Explain Millennials and Money,' *Wealthmanagement.com*, May 4, 2017
5. Tina Wadhwa, 'Millennials Are Leading the Trend on America's Hottest Investment Product,' *Business Insider*, January 24, 2017
6. Eric Bush, '10-Year Annualized Change in Personal Income Is the Slowest on Record,' *Advisor Perspectives*, January 31, 2017. Also, 'State of U.S. Wealth: More Millionaires, Bigger Wealth Divide,' *Yahoo Finance*, February 16, 2017; Gary Halbert, 'America Continues to Lead the World in Wealth by a Longshot,' *Forecasts & Trends*, March 7, 2017;

Laurence B. Siegel, 'Middle-Class Wage Stagnation Is a First-World Problem – the World is Getting Richer,' *Advisor Perspectives*, March 20, 2017; John Mauldin, 'The Influence of Affluence,' *Outside the Box*, April 2, 2017; Vincent Del Giudice and Wei Lu, 'America's Rich Get Richer and the Poor Get Replaced by Robots,' Bloomberg, April 26, 2017; and 'The Dangers of Planning on Working Longer,' *Wealth Advisor*, June 7, 2017

7. For a periodic table of investment return by classes, see 'Building Portfolios for the Long Term,' *Fidelity Investments*, March 2017

CHAPTER 7 – Playing Defense

1. Marlene S. Cooper, 'The Importance of Proper Beneficiary Designations,' *The Pasadena Journal*, January 3, 2017.

2. Melody Juge, 'Is Your Estate Plan Up to Date? Check These 5 Things,' *Market Watch*, January 12, 2017. Also, 'Does Your Estate Plan Need a Second Opinion,' *Wealth Advisor*, April 17, 2017; Andrew T. Wolfe and Martin M. Shenkman, 'SLATs Provide Flexible Plans for Many Clients,' *Wealthmanagement.com*, May 15, 2017; Alexander A. Bove, Jr., & Melissa Langa, 'Ferri v. Powell: Decanting with the Stars,' *Steve Leimberg's Estate Planning Newsletter*, June 8, 2017; and Jay Adkisson, Chris Riser, and David Slenn, 'Transfirst Group, Inc. v. Magliarditi: U.S. District Court Holds that Nevada Law Permits Piercing of Nevada LLLs, Nevada Partnerships, and Nevada Trusts,' *Steve Leimberg's Asset Protection Planning Newsletter*, June 19. 2017. For the consequences of a court-ordered reformation of an irrevocable life insurance trust, see **PLR 201723002**.

3. Robert Laura, 'Retirement's Deadly Undercurrent,' *Financial Advisor*, February 15, 2017. Also, Wouter Sturkenboom, 'Why Should We Care about Geopolitical Risk?' *Advisor Perspectives*, March 9, 2017 and George Schneider,' When Enough Is Never Enough: Four-Pocket Retirement Strategy,' *Seeking Alpha*, March 24, 2017

4. Peter Gladstone, 'On the Divorce Firing Line: HNW Executive Compensation Packages,' *Wealthmanagement.com*, February 21, 2017. Also, Lisa Brown, 'A Trust Can Protect Your Adult Child's Assets from a Failed Marriage,' *Nasdaq*, March 6, 2017 and Jeffrey A. Weissman, 'Seven Steps to Building a Better Pre-Nup,' *Wealthmanagement.com*, May 11, 2017

5. Jed Davis, 'Protecting Wealthy Clients from Cyber Attack,' *Wealthmanagement.com*, March 1, 2017. Also, Diane Jermyn, 'High-Net-Worth Lifestyle Brings Liability Tripwires,' The Globe and Mail, February 14, 2017; Ryan W. Neal, 'First State-Mandated Cybersecurity Law Goes into Effect in New York,' *Wealthmanagement.com*, March 1, 2017; and Anna Sulkin, 'Security Risks for Wealthy Families Are on the Rise,' *Wealthmanagement.com*, March 9, 2017

6. Robert Finnegan. 'Planning in Uncertain Times Part III : The Cost of Delay with Life Insurance,' *Steve Leimberg's Estate Planning Newsletter*, April 12, 2017

7. Karen Demasters, 'Even the Wealthy Worry about Health Care Costs,' *Private Wealth*, April 2017. Also, Karen Demasters, 'These States Are Ideal for Pre-Retirees,' *Financial Advisor*, June 28, 2017 and Karen Demasters, 'Advisors Must Lead on Protection of Elderly from Financial Abuse,' *Financial Advisor*, June 29, 2017

CHAPTER 8 – Playing Offense

1. For an explanation of estate freezes and other advanced strategies, see David H. Lenok, 'How Cold Assets Can Help Keep Others Hot,' *Wealthmanagement.com*, January 10, 2017. Also, Martin M. Shenkman, "Checklist: Gumby Trust,' *Shenkman Practical Planner*, January-March, 2017; Jeff Baskies, 'Estate of Kollsman: Art Discounts Are Alive and Well – Tax Court Rejects Estate's Expert's Values , but Allows Unique Discounts,' *Steve*

Leimberg's Estate Planning Newsletter, May 1, 2017; Mary P. O'Reilly and Jason Smith, 'Trust Beneficiaries Eliminated Through a Decanting Pursuant to the Trust Instrument Found Valid in New York,' *Steve Leimberg's Estate Planning Newsletter*, May 8, 2017 and Pete Melcher, Bob Keebler, and Steve Oshins, 'The Ultimate Guide to Decanting Trusts: Strategies, Opportunities, Private Decantings, Tax Issues and More,' *Steve Leimberg's Estate Planning Newsletter*, May 24, 2017

2. Russ Alan Prince, 'High-End Life Insurance Agents without an Estate Tax Become Wealth Managers,' *Forbes*, January 18, 2017. Also, 'Use an Irrevocable Life Insurance Trust as a Wealth Preserver,' *Wealth Advisor*, February 27, 2017

3. Chuck Carnevale, '12 Dividend Growth Stocks that Meet My 'Magic Formula' for Dividend Growth Investors,' *Seeking Alpha*, February 5, 2017. Also, SD Davis, 'Dividend Stocks Are (or Will Be) the Bubble in this Market Cycle,' *Seeking Alpha*, February 16, 2017 and "Retirement Strategy: The Wealth Accumulation Phase with My Simple Strategy,' *Seeking Alpha*, June 17, 2017

4. Aaron Hodari, 'Benefits and Risks of Premium Finance,' *Wealthmanagement.com*, February 23, 2017. Also, Barry Flagg, 'Essential Ingredients to Life Insurance ADVICE,' *Steve Leimberg's Estate Planning Newsletter*, May 17, 2017 and Bruce Steiner, 'Life Insurance Policy Settlement Options,' *Steve Leimberg's Estate Planning Newsletter*, June 12, 2017

5. Kevin McKinley, 'Roth IRA Tips, Tricks and Twists,' Wealthmanagement.com, February 23, 2017. Also, George Schneider, 'Never Run Out of Money: The Gift That Keeps on Giving,' *Seeking Alpha*, March 22, 2017; Mike DeWitt, 'High Earners Should Consider a 'Back-Door' Roth IRA,' CNBC, April 4, 2017; Dr. David Eifrig. Jr., 'Two Secrets and Two Dangers to a Roth IRA Conversion.' *Retirement Millionaire Daily*, April 25, 2017; and Elithea Mas, 'Five Ways Trusteed IRAs Can Keep a Good thing Going,' Wealthmanagement.com, April 24, 2107

6. Steve Oshins, 'The 20th Anniversary of Domestic Asset Protection Trusts,' *Steve Leimberg's Asset Protection Planning Newsletter*, April 3, 2017

7. Robert F. Sharpe, Jr., 'Who Makes Charitable Gifts and Why?' Wealthmanagement.com, May 18, 2017. Also, Barbara Benware, 'Charitable Planning Opportunity: Donate Private Equity Fund Interests,' *Advisor Perspectives*, May 24, 2017

8. Carole M. Bass, 'Reforming a Will for Tax Savings,' *Trusts & Estates*, May 2017

CHAPTER 9 – The Season Schedule

1. Conrad Teitell, 'Inform Clients of Reporting Requirements for Charitable Gifts,' *Wealthmanagement.com*, January 4, 2017.

2. David L. Silvian and Phyllis Maloney Johnson, 'Do Trustees Have a Duty to Consider Decanting?' *Wealthmanagement.com*, April 25, 2017. Also, Martin M. Shenkman, 'Old Irrevocable Trust Makeover,' *Shenkman Practical Planner*, April-June 2017.

3. John McManus, 'Ten Estate Planning Strategies While Waiting for Tax Reform,' *Wealthmanagement.com*, May 12, 2017.

4. David R. York and Andrew L. Howell, 'Pushing Wealth transfer Plans Into the 21st Century,' *Wealthmanagement.com*, May 12, 2017.

5. Ken Steiner, 'A Proven Way to Budget Clients' Spending,' *Advisor Perspectives*, May 29, 2017.

6. To secure an extension of time to make an Alternate Valuation election, see **PLR 201719014**.

7.   Dawn S. Markowitz, 'IRS Not Time-Barred From Collecting Estate Taxes,' *Wealthmanagement.com*, June 7, 2017. Also, Kevin A. Diehl, 'Who Controls How Voluntary Payments to IRS Are Applied?' *Wealthmanagement.com*, June 1, 2017.

CHAPTER 10 – Fouls and Penalties

1.   Robert W. Cockren, Thomas G. Opferman, etal., 'How Do Recent Updates to Estate Laws Impact Your Future?' Lexology, February 24, 2017.
2.   Dana Anspach, 'Hidden Estate Planning Mistakes That Have Horrible Consequences,' *MarketWatch*, March 6, 2017.
3.   'Baby Boomers May Be Putting Their Family's Inheritances at Risk, *ResponseSource*, March 13, 2017.
4.   Matthew Wallace, 'Protecting Your Assets from Your Spouse,' *The Times Herald*, February 24, 2017.
5.   Porter Stansberry, 'Would You Lend $1 Trillion to a Bunch of 18-Year-Olds?' *The Crux*, April 18, 2017.
6.   For a sobering view of the state and effect of government pensions in the United States, see John Mauldin, 'Angst in America, Part 5: The Crisis We Can't Muddle Through,' *Thoughts from the Frontline*, April 23, 2017.
7.   Jillian Merns, 'Appeals Court Disallows Deduction for Interest on Loan,' *Wealthmanagement.com*, May 9, 2017.

CHAPTER 11 – Distractions

1.   'Scary Headlines Can Lead to Restless Investors,' *Nationwide*, February 21, 2017
2.   Patrick Watson, 'How to Survive the Obamacare Collapse,' *Connecting the Dots*, March 28, 2017
3.   Anna Sulkin, 'How to Prevent Feuds between Heirs,' *Wealthmanagement.com*, April 10, 2017
4.   Jim Counts, 'Is the IRS Helping Identity Thieves Access Taxpayer information?' *Steve Leimberg's Income Tax Planning Newsletter*, April 19, 2017
5.   'Will a Robot Take Your Job?' *Wealth Advisor*, April 24, 2017
6.   George Schneider, 'Which of these 6 Investing Mistakes Will You Make?' *Seeking Alpha*, May 12, 2017
7.   Chris Taylor, 'How to Keep Your Clients Safe from Fake Financial News?' *Reuters*, May 17, 2017

CHAPTER 12 – Conclusions

NO additional materials

Webinars and Presentations

In addition to end notes, the period from late 2016 through June 30, 2017 was accompanied by a number of high-level webinars and presentations. While many of these would be considered 'too complicated' for many people, they do, in fact, represent the best single opportunity to note the major trends and issues that apply to some of the issues covered in *Playing the Game*. As such, I have also included these for your benefit. In some cases, accessing these materials might require the assistance of a third party (accountant, attorney, financial advisor); however, if you have the desire to understand what's happening today and how professionals are addressing issues and questions, these webinars and presentations are some of the best and most complete sources of data. For your benefit, I have listed these in alphabetical order by topic.

'Collaboration: It's Not a Four Letter Word,' presented by Martin M. Shenkman.

'Compilation of Meeting Notes from Heckerling 2017,' *Steve Leimberg's Estate Planning Email Newsletter* presented by Martin M. Shenkman

'Decanting an Irrevocable Trust: The 'Do-Over' Trust,' *Premier Trust,* presented by Steven J. Oshins and Brian J. Simmons.

'Deconstructing Conflict: Understanding Family Business Shared Wealth and Power, *Trusts & Estates*, presented by Doug Daumoel and Blair Trippe.

'Embracing the Digital Revolution: How to Empower Digital Advice to Create Scale,' presented by *Envestnet*.

'42nd Annual Notre Dame Tax & Estate Planning Institute: Highlights,' presented by Martin M. Shenkman.

'4 Ways – Connecting with the Next Generation of Investors,' presented by *SS&C Advent*.

'HNWI's Vision for the Wealth Management Industry in the Information Age,' presented by *Factset*.

'Modern Goals: Behavioral Strategies for Long-Term Success,' *Morningstar*, presented by Sarah Newcombe.

'Planning Considerations for the Post-Nuclear Family,' *Trusts & Estates* and *St Jude Children's Research Hospital*, presented by Bobbi J. Bierhals and Kim Kamin.

'Pre and Post-Nup Clauses to Address Trust Issues,' presented by Martin M. Shenkman and Rebecca Provder.

'Spousal Lifetime Access Trusts – Key Planning Tool' presented by Martin M. Shenkman and David H. Kirk.

'10 Best Estate Planning Strategies in 2017,' presented by Robert S. Keebler and Steven J. Oshins.

'Trump Tax Plan,' *Leimberg Information Services*, presented by Robert S. Keebler.

'Trust: Planning and Drafting for Divorce,' presented by Rebecca Provder, Gideon Rothschild, and Martin M. Shenkman.

'2016 Connect Investor Report: Insights into the Advisor-Investor Relationship,' presented by *salesforce research*.

'Wealth Management Perspectives,' presented by Morgan Stanley.

About the Author

Paul T. Remack has spent the last 35 years as a financial planner, founding two companies and helping more than 200 affluent families, many over multiple generations, navigate the challenges of ever-changing and dynamic economic environments. He is a Certified Financial Planner, a Certified Professional Fiduciary and was awarded a Masters degree in Taxation. Paul also pursued a Ph.D. in Renaissance History. He lives in California with his wife, Linda, and their cat, Gracie.

Morgan James
Speakers Group

↗ www.TheMorganJamesSpeakersGroup.com

We connect Morgan James published
authors with live and online events
and audiences who will benefit
from their expertise.

CPSIA information can be obtained
at www.ICGtesting.com
Printed in the USA
LVHW041201041218
599214LV00006B/8/P